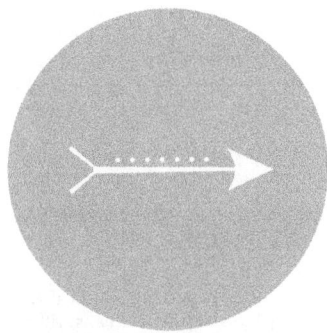

DISCLAIMER

The material in this publication is of the nature of general comment only and does not represent professional advice. It is not intended to provide specific guidance for any particular circumstances, and it should not be relied upon for any decision to take action or not to take action on any matter which it covers. Readers should obtain professional advice, where appropriate, before making any such decision. To the maximum extent permitted by law, the author and publisher disclaim all responsibility and liability to any person, whether arising directly or indirectly, from any person taking or not taking action based on the information in this book.

National Library of Australia Cataloguing-in-Publication entry
Title: The Adversity Advantage
Subtitle: Increase Your Leadership Adaptability.
Mastering the Scenario Thinking Framework™
ISBN: 978-0-646-99957-9 (paperback)
ISBN: 978-0-646-80242-8 (ebook)
Subjects: Business, communication, leadership.

Book photographs:
"Dongfeng" VOR yacht and Volvo Ocean Race 2017/18 trophy-
Carolijn Brouwer - Trimmer, photographs by Eloi Stichelbaut
"The Daily Telegraph" yacht Round Britain & Ireland Race 2003,
photograph by "Beken of Cowes", and trophy Claudia Lantos - crew,
own photograph
"The Mistake": 18 ft skiff classics race, in which Claudia Lantos crewed
on in 2012, own photograph

Book Illustrations: Claudia Lantos
Lantos Logo design: Loed van Berkel, Van Berkel Marketing & Communicatie
Book Coach & Project Management: Kath Walters
Project Management team: editors and proofreaders Jess Horton and Gail Seymour
Cover and internal design: Liz Seymour, Seymour Design
Cover photograph: Chris Gleisner, Chris Gleisner Photography
Hair stylist, cover photo: Antler Hair Designs, Bondi Beach: Yui, Hayley & Jasmine
Printed and bound by IngramSpark.

THE ADVERSITY ADVANTAGE

INCREASE YOUR LEADERSHIP ADAPTABILITY

>·······→

MASTERING THE
SCENARIO THINKING FRAMEWORK™

CLAUDIA LANTOS

Lantos

A LANTOS COACHING & CONSULTANCY PUBLICATION

PRAISE FOR *THE ADVERSITY ADVANTAGE*

"With *The Adversity Advantage*, Claudia Lantos has written a very generous book that shares profound and helpful insights from her (clearly very impactful) coaching practice. There are enough simple and yet powerful tips, tricks and life 'hacks' in this book to make a first reading very worthwhile for anyone trying to navigate the modern workplace, and some bigger ideas and useful tools that warrant a second reading."

Mandy Geddes, General Manager, Education, IECL by GrowthOps

"Claudia's book really resonated with me as it took me back to the many adversities I faced in my own life. In *The Adversity Advantage*, Claudia addresses some of the most compelling realities and needs of our times. Like the alchemist that turns lead into gold, Claudia's Scenario Thinking Framework™ offers a process to turn adversity into adaptability and resilience. This book is an essential read for coaches, managers and leaders."

Sebastian Salicru, Business Psychologist, Professional Certified Coach (PCC) and Author of *Leadership Results*

"*The Adversity Advantage* reminds you there's always a different way to look at a seemingly immovable situation in front of you. Claudia has provided a number of practical tools and tips to help do just that."

Edwina Waddy

"Claudia's narrative is accessible and practical. Her story is peppered with excellent examples throughout enabling the reader to relate and make sense of her messages. The distinction between High Performer and High Achiever is thought provoking and I look forward to exploring one of Claudia's key messages more for myself, 'only accept the status quo that is right for you.'"

Jane Porter, Head of Coaching and Education People & Leadership, GrowthOps and IECL by GrowthOps

"I am delighted that Claudia has decided to share her insight and experience with all people who wish to develop themselves, by writing this book. Claudia's unique ability to give intense focus on goals she sets for herself and get inspiration from long term targets is truly inspirational.

In her book she combines personal encounters with adversity with the broader scope of challenges managers encounter in personal and professional life. A smooth read, with valuable take-aways."

Karin Koks - van der Sluijs, Non-executive and supervisory board member global real-estate

"Being in Executive Search myself I especially liked the part where high achievers are coached to become high performers. I also acknowledge that coaching is no longer a method to fix somebody's shortcomings, but nowadays seen as a reward, using Executive Coaching to do even better."

Ludo Houben, Owner Houben Executive Search

"Only accept the status quo that's right for you."

For my Dad and fellow high achiever

ACKNOWLEDGEMENTS

Anything worthwhile is never accomplished alone, it's always teamwork. I've had so much fun sharing this journey with those close to me. I could never have written this book without the ongoing support of my loving, overseas family, especially my mum, sister Manuela and niece Roos.

And of course, the support of my closest friends (you know who you are) who have encouraged me along the way, and kept me sane throughout the process of writing, alongside growing my executive coaching business. Without your humour and words of wisdom it wouldn't have been much fun. Who knows, maybe this book will become famous one day and then we definitely will walk the red carpet together, Maureen Bremer.

This new journey started with creating a new logo, fine-tuning my niche further as a coach: Thank you Loed van Berkel, for the great and fun conversations, for telling me "how it's done" and finding a shark that truly represents my brand and personality. Thank you lovely Megan Tait, for your support and encouraging me to share my adversity stories to empower others. And many thanks to the "LANTOS dream team" for turning my book idea into reality: Kath Walters, my book coach, you approached me with perfect timing to write my book. Thanks so much for your patience, strict processes, creativity and guidance. We are both finishers and I will not keep you a secret. Thanks to Liz Seymour, for totally getting me and translating that into an amazing book cover and layout design, and thanks for your ongoing support and great ideas. Thanks to Maz Farrelly for being an inspiration and thinking with me and introducing me to the awesome photographer Chris Gleisner. Chris, I really enjoyed our Bondi Beach photo shoot and will have photos from that for years to come.

Thanks to (Simon) Keijzer. Great to catch up here in Bondi and for introducing me to sailing royalty Carolijn Brouwer. It's always nice to meet fellow Dutchies in Oz, especially when we share the love of offshore sailing. Carolijn, I enjoyed our conversations very much and especially your stories of adversity, peak performance and winning.

Thank you, Wil Tran, for helping me develop my website. Thank you, Mark Burton for helping me shift through the many words that later became the foundation for my positioning. And thanks to Joost de Boer, for helping me with my improved website 2.0. Thank you, Richard Burton, for being my coach and friend, ever since I came to Australia, helping me with navigating through the several crossroads I encountered. Thank you, Liz Burrows, for providing your support and being there for me.

And many thanks to everyone who has helped me to grow along the way and made executive coaching such a wonderful and fascinating profession to work in.

A big thank you to my proof readers, for your friendship, valuable time, feedback, support and shared anticipation leading up to the book launch: The fabulous Edwina Waddy, Mandy Geddes, Sebastian Salicru, Jane Porter, Karin Koks - van der Sluijs and Ludo Houben. And last but certainly not least, this book couldn't exist without the many wonderful collaborations I have had with my clients and coachees over the years, both in The Netherlands and in Australia. The examples that I have used are common themes. Don't worry that you can recognise yourself, as the examples are taken from a 12-year period and apply to more than two or three people. Yes, they are truly universal themes. You have inspired me in so many ways and I have learned and grown so much from our time together, both as a coach and as a human being, thank you so much. Looking forward to continuing to work together and to keep on growing, learning and evolving as the best coach and friend I can be for you all.

CONTENTS

INTRODUCTION

WHY READ A BOOK ABOUT ADVERSITY?

et me take you back to how my adversity at a young age has shaped me. You might relate to it. I left home aged 17 to provide for myself, finishing high school and going into University after that. So, in an accelerated way, I learned to make my own life decisions at a young age. I learned to deal with things thrown at me at school and University and figure out my professional pathway and to financially get by. I always was a quite independent and entrepreneurial spirit and very much valued my freedom.

Some three years after starting my career in 1993 as a lawyer in a big law firm in The Netherlands, I realised I couldn't apply my entrepreneurial spirit. When I left, my peers all thought I was very brave to make such a move. I started at a global UK-listed professional services group where I got to thrive. In the following eight years, while I was working there, I was given several opportunities to build new market areas. First as a sole contributor, and later as a manager in both Singapore and in Amsterdam, opening up new markets and building small teams from scratch. When I moved to Singapore and asked for advice how I should deal with the Singapore market, the COO of our group just said: "Oh, you'll figure it out." That appealed to my entrepreneurial spirit and desire for autonomy, and I loved the opportunity to set up and establish a pilot for the group, growing it into a new business offering. However, around 2003, when I had the chance to also build up the new business offering in Amsterdam, my professional adversity materialised in the form of the negative 9/11 effects on the market. That forced me and my team to join the companies' other existing businesses, joining other existing teams. I had to stop growing and building the new business offering in Amsterdam, which I had also set up in Singapore, and which was the reason for me moving back home. I had always been in high achiever mode and used to be listed amongst the highest fee earners, so joining one of the existing teams didn't appeal to me and made me reflect. Was this what I wanted and when I was at my best?

My following career moves in employment were again entrepreneurial in setting up new parts of the business. And in 2005, I was ready to continue my career setting up my own consultancy business in executive search and executive coaching. First in The Netherlands for eight years and after that in Australia.

I gained some knowledge and experience on adversity myself, both in my personal and working life. I learned even more from people I worked with throughout my career, about how they dealt with adversity and how they turned it into an advantage.

We all face adversity in some form during our life and career. And the timing of it is never right. "Is adversity ever welcome?" you might ask yourself. And no, I'm not a fluffy person who would say: "Everything happens for a reason." Yet when we turn our adversity into an advantage, when we make it work for us and use the insights and learnings to their fullest, at least it has not been wasted on us and we can turn it into something positive. The upside is, we can use the adversity to become more effective as a leader, increase our adaptability and resilience, and from that recognise and deal with adversity much faster in future.

I certainly have experienced this first hand, with five car accidents and four concussions over a period of about 10 years. During that time, I set up new business areas when I was employed, started my own coaching business twice and moved twice to the other side of the world. Ironically, the last concussion happened last week, when I was wrapping up the final text for this book. So, I can now fine-tune and apply my own learnings again and come out stronger.

In this fast-paced and ever-changing, complex world we live in, we all need to constantly increase our leadership adaptability and resilience, especially when things don't go as planned.

The leaders I work with in my coaching practice have a tough challenge managing their own performance and that of their teams, while dealing with peers, bosses and other internal and external stakeholders driving their business both operationally and strategically. They deal with changing market environments, demanding clients, high pressure and workloads, all whilst keeping fit and healthy and finding time to spend with family and friends. That's no mean feat. They are not always used to asking for help. They often believe that they should be able to fulfil their role on their own with no outside help and that they should know what to do. Getting that support to bounce ideas off someone is sometimes an emotional release. For some people, only then do they fully realise how tough they had it. Dealing with adversity in either your personal or professional life has become just another, albeit tough, part of the job. Wouldn't it be great to be able to turn the adversity you encounter as a leader to your advantage?

As an executive coach, my purpose is to help you thrive in your role as a leader, instead of suffering, pushing through and surviving. Let adversity work for you. I'm very much motivated to help you put the least effort in, get the best possible outcomes, and make your life easier. That's why I have combined all my learnings from my 20-plus years' career in professional services working with some amazing, inspiring leaders, on how to turn adversity into an advantage, and especially to do that in an accelerated way.

I especially focus on working with high achievers, helping them to manage their peak performance. That's where my strengths have the most added value and where we find synergy, speaking the same language as soon as possible. The funny thing is, most high achievers don't consider themselves a high achiever. Working hard and getting the best results and achieving goals is normal for them. You know you are a high achiever when you strive to achieve goals, have high standards, are hard on yourself and strive for high performance.

However, we are all human and no one is perfect. No one is a high performer all the time. Simply put, we regularly shift from being a high performer—an effective leader and role model, involving people around us in our journeys—to being a high achiever—laser focused, driven to achieve a certain goal, prone to losing sight of the bigger picture, pushing through even when the going gets tough, facing adversity. Most often, this comes at a great cost: building frustration due to lack of progress, lack of creativity or productivity, lack of buy in from peers, and pressure mounting, lack of time to delegate well. At some point, exhaustion sets in and mistakes are made.

I focus on helping people shift from "high achiever" to "high performer" mode when it's needed, because I recognise myself in them. I've had some tough commercial goals in my career where I wanted to be the best and needed to be in the top rankings—not so much to compete with other people, but to get the best out of myself. I've experienced the cost that it can come with, and the knowledge that it can be so much better.

HOW OR WHY CAN I HELP YOU WITH THE ADVERSITY YOU ENCOUNTER?

Being in my early fifties now, I have accumulated so many insights from the leaders that I've worked with during my career. I'm keen to share some of those best practices with people who have the same DNA makeup. I've seen the leaders I work with move from just surviving, to thriving and empowering others. Their accelerated learning curve is contagious for the people around them, and I want everyone to experience it.

Ever since my father passed in June 2018 (who also was a typical high achiever), I've focused my energy even more on finding and articulating my niche and helping leaders to be the best they can be, whilst dealing with all kinds of adversity. Life is too short to be stuck and to procrastinate on how to deal with things that don't go your way, especially as those "things" nowadays are mostly unprecedented. And I now know I have found my niche. Ever since I was able to articulate my niche better, I found people relate better to me, recognising their own story. I attract more of the right clients and coachees and have been more successful in my area.

And not many people consider adversity for what it is: a setback, or something that doesn't go as planned, and that it's best to deal with that head on (as you will learn in this book) in the most effective and methodical way.

Would you like to make your life easier for yourself and others around you, being more effective as a leader? If yes, then this book is for you. I've written it especially for leaders in an ever-changing and fast-paced environment, facing adversity. I want to make their lives easier by helping them to be more reflective and create more choices whilst facing adversity.

My book is for anyone who recognises that for themselves. I'm passionate about this topic, because it can be such an eye-opener. I like to surprise people with what they're capable of and how things can be more effortless and fun.

Acting with curiosity, passion and purpose gets you a long way. Find your intrinsic motivation and keep evolving by connecting the dots and recognising patterns, solving problems effectively along the way.

How? There's not one set answer. Anything worthwhile is never easy to achieve. But the tools and real life business examples I have gathered for you in this book will definitely help you with that. Especially mastering the Scenario Thinking Framework™, my signature tool I have developed over many years working closely with high achievers.

The overarching message of this book is: If things don't go your way, don't dwell on it; take action. My motto has always been: "Only accept the status quo that's right for you." Then you will increase your ability to be effective and efficient in decision-making, and to be resilient. I want to help people who are highly driven and highly active in their careers to stop and reflect on the situation they're facing and make a reflective decision whether it's right for them, instead of pushing through and hoping for better times. Hope is not a strategy. Action and adaption are the only change agents.

WHAT'S COMING UP?

In this book, I'm talking about how you can turn adversity into an advantage, and how it's not always bad to have adversity. It's full of learnings, and it will make your life easier in future—helping you to thrive and not just survive. I will introduce to you a tool I've created—the Scenario Thinking Framework™—which will help you to navigate through adversity in business with more adaptability in both decision-making and your resilience.

I'll also talk about the differences between a High Achiever and a High Performer, and how you can shift from one state to the other to help you to be more effective. I'll share with you how to manage and maintain your peak performance because you can control that more than you think. If you control your mind, you can control your performance—as shown by the elite athlete that I also interview in this section.

I'll explain how you can best regain perspective and how to reset. Sometimes we do need to reset when things get too complex or when we get overwhelmed. It's always good to be aware where you stand and how you can move on more effectively.

With that, it's all about using your strengths. I take you through strengths management, over-use and under-use of your strengths, and how we can be our most authentic selves.

Last but not least, I'll provide you with some neuroscience hacks and show you how to trick your brain to set yourself up for success.

One of the big gifts of adversity is that it makes us reflect. When everything is going our way, we just power through. When we encounter enough adversity to make us stop and think, and we use the tools I'll be giving you throughout this book, we come out stronger and clearer. I feel enriched by my experiences with adversity, which is why I wrote this book—I want to share my wisdom with others and help you to see that my methods will work for you too.

THE ADVERSITY
ADVANTAGE

INTRODUCTION

How on earth is adversity an advantage? Although nobody normally welcomes adversity, it is a topic close to my heart. Let me take you on a journey and show you that using adversity from business or life events is a powerful advantage for leadership effectiveness. It will increase your leadership adaptability and accelerate your decision making. Especially in combination with mastering my self-developed, signature tool, The Scenario Thinking Framework™, which I'm excited to introduce to you in Chapter 2.

I wrote this book because I realised that some of the leaders I came across in my 12-plus years as an executive coach in leadership development are passionate about their role but not always thriving in it. When the going gets tough, they sometimes stop having fun or enjoying the role. It seems they are then more surviving or on autopilot. I don't think that is ideal, do you?

I love helping leaders to enjoy and excel at what they set out to do rather than just getting through. Didn't you take up that leadership role to make a positive difference, and impact on the business? Didn't you want to role model the desired culture, way of working and effective behaviours to the rest of the organisation, to amplify those outcomes for others? Wouldn't you want to feel your best and perform your best?

Let me surprise you with what you are capable of.

By the end of this book, I hope to have encouraged and empowered you to recognise the difference between just getting through and being at your best. I'm keen to share with you what it looks like to optimise your strengths using some powerful neuroscience hacks, and how to thrive at peak performance.

WHAT IS ADVERSITY IN BUSINESS AND WHY IS IT IMPORTANT TO FLAG AND UNDERSTAND ADVERSITY?

In this chapter, I am going to explain what I mean by adversity, why it's important to flag and understand that first sign of adversity, and how you can use it to your advantage. I'll show you how this adversity can strengthen you, and the advantages or benefits of this experience. I will share some of my own and others' adverse experiences, and how they resulted in me being so much more adaptable and effective, with an increased quality of life.

WHAT IS ADVERSITY?

Let me start by sharing with you the meaning of adversity you'll find in various dictionaries, and online, and then provide you with my own interpretation for this book.

The Cambridge Dictionary defines adversity thus:

"Adversity is a difficult or unlucky situation or event." I specifically like the example they mention: "The road to happiness is paved with adversity." Which is so true.

In general, the meaning of adversity is: bad luck, misfortune, trouble, difficulty, hardship, suffering, pain, and even torture. It's an event that's not working for you, that is not beneficial.

Specifically, in business, adversity shows up when your efforts are not going to plan, when hurdles or setbacks get in the way of your goals or desired situation. Adversity may appear in the form of a difficult working relationship with your boss, peers, direct reports, stakeholders. It could be that you have different working styles or approaches, different communication styles or leadership styles, or conflicting objectives or priorities, and deadlines. Or it could be a lack of budget or resources or market disruption.

There are so many ways you can face adversity in business. A temporary feeling of overwhelm or lack of self-belief or confidence can show up. But adversity can also show up in your private life and have a significant impact on your working life. Adversity, in short, is a situation we would rather not be in. And we need to find a way to deal with it and come out stronger.

Here is how I define adversity for my clients: "A status quo that's not right for you."

If you find yourself in a situation of adversity, a situation that doesn't work for you, don't ignore it or linger too long to deal with it: "Only accept the status quo that's right for you."

The truth is that adversity always serves a purpose, although it's not clear straight away. Surprisingly, adversity can be hard to identify and become aware of. We are so busy trying to fight it that we just think of it as "this is my reality" or "the status quo." But the more you practice recognising adversity, the faster you get at dealing with it head on, the more you'll figure out how to face adversity sooner every time. From that awareness, you'll reinvent yourself faster and more effortlessly move in a new direction and set sail on another course.

MY ADVENTURES IN ADVERSITY

I have been a bit unlucky with accidents. Let me explain what happened and what the silver lining was for me personally and in business and, fast forwarding, for the leaders I work with.

Over a period of 10 years, which started in 1998, I had five similar car accidents, all hit from behind by another car and not my mistake. And twice I wasn't even driving, but a passenger in a taxi and in a friend's car. The very first accident alone took me nine months to fully recover. I was driving myself on the highway and travelling at about a 100kph. It was Friday evening, and everyone was trying to get home for the weekend. I came over a rise after going uphill and, unfortunately, drove into a chain collision on the downhill. I had to hit the brakes suddenly, and the person coming behind me, of course, didn't see the light of my brakes and hit me almost at full speed. My car turned into an accordion (it was crumpled) and I was hit so hard from behind that I doubled over forwards and then backward, fast. Although luckily my spine was intact, the accident stretched all the muscles around it from my neck to lower back. I was in a job where I had to drive about 60,000km per year visiting clients, so I had to adapt whilst recovering to keep my job, and keep the business I was responsible for, going.

What is more, I had another four car accidents in the years after, which also took some recovery. And coupled with that on separate occasions, I had three accidents while sailing yachts, each of which resulted in a concussion.

The last concussion, in 2012, was quite severe. It was the kind of personal adversity that affected my professional life a lot. I had just moved to Australia by myself at 44 years old. After only a couple of months in my new job, I had the sailing accident that left me severely concussed.

I was still on probation. I had a working visa, and my contract only allowed me 10 sick days. I had no financial backup to take leave. So, I pushed through my severe concussion, which obviously took its toll. I recognised I was in the midst of adversity, but I didn't see any solution other than to push through at the time. As a result, that concussion ended up taking much longer to get over. It took me two and a half years to overcome the daily, chronic headaches, fatigue and concentration, and limited energy issues.

The impact at the time was that I didn't have much energy other than for work. My social life was non-existent and my stress levels high. So, you might say I was more "surviving" than "thriving."

But something good came out of it. After all that, I promised myself I would do things differently, making sure that all this adversity had a silver lining.

The boat, an 18ft classic skiff was called "The Mistake" on which I had a severe concussion, that took me 2.5yrs to recover from. Should have known better.
PHOTOGRAPH FROM OWN COLLECTION

The 72ft yacht I was on as crew during The Round Britain & Ireland Race 2003. This was during the start at the Needles, at sea close to the Isle of Wight, United Kingdom, sailing in about 30 knots of wind.
PHOTOGRAPH BY BEKEN OF COWES OF "THE DAILY TELEGRAPH"

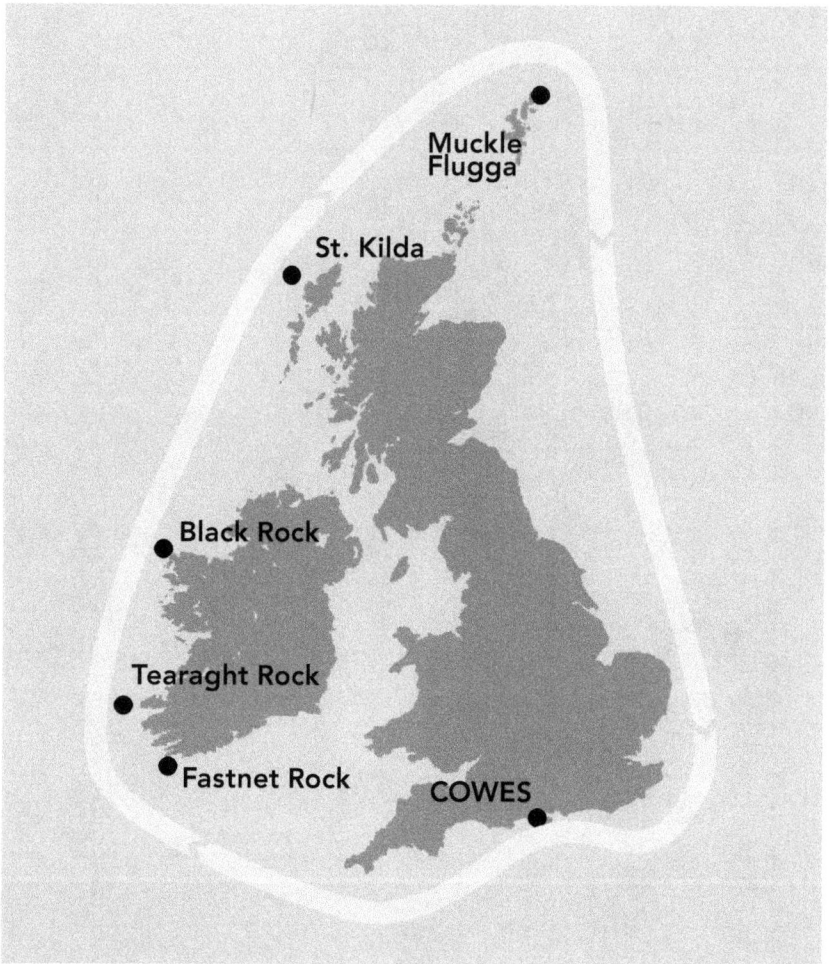

The 1,805 nautical miles/2,077 miles route and direction
of "the Round Britain and Ireland Race" 2003
ILLUSTRATION FROM WWW.ROUNDBRITAINANDIRELAND.RORC.ORG

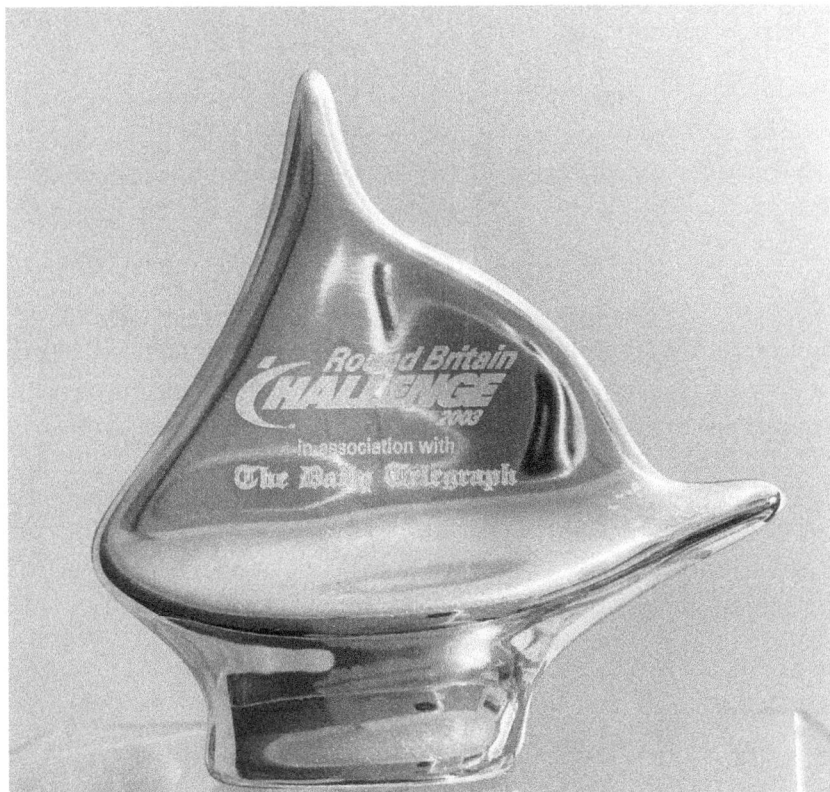

My individual trophy for 3rd place in "The Round Britain and Ireland Race", as a crew member on "The Daily Telegraph" a 72-foot yacht in 2003.
PHOTOGRAPH FROM OWN COLLECTION

The adversity I see happening in the lives of my clients can be both personal and professional. It's so vital to recognise when you need to change tactics, apply another approach and get creative to get back into your peak performance.

Today, my own experiences and those of my clients of bouncing back, are still a source of inspiration and resilience for me. I'm driven to turn adversity into an advantage for the leaders I work with and help them to reflect on why it happened and what the learnings are. Big life events make you think.

Adversity has definitely enabled me to reinvent myself several times to my advantage. These events weren't appreciated as an advantage in business at first, but later on, they developed into an advantageous mindset and approach to tackle almost anything that was thrown at me successfully.

In his book *Awaken the Giant Within*, Tony Robbins says, "How we deal with adversity in challenges will shape our lives more than almost anything else." Adversity comes in all shapes and sizes. My personal and professional adversities gave me a chance to reflect on how I dealt with them.

Another example of where you can encounter adversity is in sports. I'd always been interested in competitive sailing, but never had proper training. Yet I signed up for a massive off-shore sailing race that I came across described in an article in the magazine *Yachting World*, in which they invited people to be selected for the race. All went well and after about six weekends of tough training, I participated in the 2003 "The Round Britain and Ireland Race," a true challenge for me. I was crew on one of the 12 one-design yachts and we each had nine people on deck, nine below, rotating in four-hour shifts. Before this race, I had only been cruising on yachts with friends, so I had to learn fast. To prepare for the race, we had six training weekends from Southampton in the lead up to the race, to make sure that we were all aligned as a team, as we didn't know each other before. For me, it was the first time I had done serious, competitive sailing and it was full on. Early morning boot camps on the Isle of Wight, learning both theory and practice of being crew on such a yacht. Then the race itself. It was a fiercely fought, nonstop two-week long race against the currents and prevailing winds over a course of 1,805 nautical miles, about 2,077 normal miles. It was in the UK Spring, in late March, early April 2003. In that part of the world, that is pretty cold. And we had all types of weather during those two weeks when we raced around Britain. Most of it was grey, cold and a bit miserable, and even a storm at one point, when we rounded the Shetland Islands. It was both a mental and physical test, in freezing conditions and no land in sight for 30 miles. At some point I was working with my designated buddy on the bow, trying to do a sail change, and we were at times knee deep in water, because of choppy seas. We had agreed, in a situation like that, that it's important that your buddy helps you to secure your line to the boat when you are moving position. When I checked my line, I discovered my buddy hadn't secured me and was now moving towards the rear of the boat. I felt very vulnerable, left to my own devices and even at risk, but I was able to quickly attach my line again. At that moment I had never felt a stronger sense of what good teamwork and communication is all about. Needless to say, nothing bad happened to either of us, but it could have gone very wrong.

It was specifically this experience, being part of a diverse team with different strengths and personalities that gave me so many insights and learnings on how to deal with adversity in life and business and build resilience, which I'm still using today. The car accidents, the concussions and the sailing race all inspired me to write this book. Because without it, I wouldn't be who I am today. And I'm sure you had your share of adversity. Everyone has.

There are countless celebrities in sport and media, who always inspire me, including top tennis player Rafael Nadal. He is ranked world number two at 32 years of age, yet has suffered many injuries. He still deals with adversity head-on and always comes back, and is still going strong at the major Grand Slam events. Or movie stars like Robert Downey Jr., who dealt with addiction and an abusive father, or Keanu Reeves, who dealt with adversity like the death of a friend, his wife and his dog. Both Robert and Keanu went on to star in many blockbuster movies. And what about well-known ex-CEO of Apple, Steve Jobs. He started the company in a garage and later found himself ousted from his company but came back and drove the business again to new heights. Also, strong women like Arianna Huffington, who went against the established media order and Oprah Winfrey, who had an abusive youth and started her business from scratch. Look where she ended up. What I admire and what inspires me is that these people don't let adversity define them or get in their way of having a successful path in life and career. It's their determination, grit, resilience, creativity and the adaptability they show. And if they didn't have the adversity, they might not have become so successful and they wouldn't have had such a compelling story to tell. I think the secret of their success, in short, is how they dealt with the adversity, looking to constantly finetune and improve their situation and those of others, and make things better.

Fast forward again to this book: my aim here is to help leaders with adversity in business, and show how they can deal with it in the most effective way. That's how I like to translate it. When it's about real life—your life—there's an even a steeper learning curve to that better approach because you don't have a choice except to deal with it. My main take away from the adversities I've faced has been that you've got to increase your adaptability in resilience just to be better prepared for the future.

When you know how to flag and understand adversity in your life, it makes you so much more effective, enjoying your job and strengthening you. However small the hurdle or setback is in business, don't let things linger; you can do something about it. Adversity in business can have a massive impact on you and other's mood and success. As a leader, you are a role model.

In the next chapters I'll provide you with tools to face the music head-on, bounce back and reinvent yourself. The faster you set a new course, the faster your team will follow suit. Just hoping for better times or keeping your head down is not a strategy. It will usually not improve your situation. Hard work, focus and some compromising or sacrificing in other areas might be needed. Great progress and success don't just happen overnight, and you will appreciate it all the more when all your hard work pays off.

With my car accidents, I just ploughed on through and that wasn't a great strategy. This was my first encounter with severe adversity of a physical nature and I basically did everything wrong. What I've learned since is to make a more substantial effort to do it right. Investing time in ways to get back to peak performance, learning from your mistakes and being more effective going forward will also enable you to contribute to the business bottom line for the longer term.

In my executive coaching practice, the adversity I come across might be that a much-anticipated promotion goes to someone else, or competitors in the market close a deal that you wanted, or your team get demotivated and are not operating as a high-performance team anymore. You may need to train new people if there's a high turnover, with loss of knowledge when they leave. You may be stuck with low engagement, and you might not make your budget. But adversity also shows up if you can't seem to find a way to deal with your new boss, or a peer, who seems to communicate differently and value other priorities or ways of working. Their personality or approach could prove to be a hurdle to get things done, and it's not always easy to work out how to best deal with them. These adversities can add up quickly and may seem daunting to handle at first, next to your already high workload and pressure. But all of that will provide you heightened awareness and insights. Introspection or reflection with a coach or mentor to help you, and taking stock of the situation that you're in, will help you recognise adversity sooner in future and you will be more confident that you can deal with it. The best part is that you will take action sooner.

Without adversity, there wouldn't be that accelerated learning and it wouldn't have improved your decision making or problem-solving skills. In Chapter 4 you will learn that applying your learnings from adversity, very much benefits you to get into your peak performance, as peak performance is an extremely efficient and effective decision-making strategy.

SOMETIMES THE TIMING FOR ADVERSITY IS JUST RIGHT

To illustrate an adversity situation in business, around 2010, one of my coachees was having a difficult relationship with his boss, which impacted his performance. He tried some new approaches, but later realised he probably had outgrown his role. So, my coachee decided to change course and go and chase his dream of traveling and working abroad. He felt he took control of his life and had increased confidence and resilience because of it. After his travels, he was refreshed and inspired and became quite successful in his career, landing roles and opportunities he couldn't have even imagined before. But it took that adversity, that difficult relationship with his boss, to show him the new direction.

Well, you might be thinking, we all know what adversity is. But often I experience that leaders don't recognise a storm until they are right in the middle of it. I usually work with high achievers and high performing leaders in my coaching practice. They all got to where they are today in challenging leadership roles through the hard work they put in and the many learnings they've had from all sorts of adversity. But what I notice more and more often, is that people think they can hold onto all their old approaches or what they know. However, the market is fast changing through digital disruption and AI. You need to be able to keep reinventing yourself proactively, set a new course and adapt and be agile and resilient, because the old approach doesn't cut it anymore. And the more senior you get, the more it's about soft skills, inclusion, and a holistic view. You need to allow yourself time to be more creative and strategic.

And of course, it depends what you want out of life. But if you are anything like me, and like to improve your life on a regular basis, be the best you can be and be very effective at work, then you'll benefit from identifying your adversity sooner.

To tackle adversity sooner, the only way for change and progress or improvement of the status quo is proactive action. Don't stay on autopilot but make it a habit to reset regularly (see more in Chapter 5). When you find yourself stuck or addressing the same issues repeatedly or procrastinating more in your life, take action. When you feel your confidence is decreasing and frustration increasing, it's time to flag that the status quo isn't right for you. Something isn't working well. And occasionally, we sense adversity early on. What you can do is to take stock of how things are going and what's important to you. Or check in with a coach and reflect on the goals you set, how you're tracking and what the effect is so far.

Adjust to the new situation, the adversity at hand, and articulate how the goals need to shift or how the approach to get there needs to shift. As a leader, you can't afford not to have a strategy in place for when things change. Taking action can start by taking some small steps. It's like when the sails are flapping whilst sailing, it means the boat is off course. So, you need to set another course or readjust the sails. You can't wait with that. Otherwise, you end up somewhere else and sometimes you need to tack, to get that smooth sailing back.

If you don't identify the adversity as such and you're not willing to do any reflection or introspection, then you find yourself stuck, knowing something's wrong but you can't put your finger on what. That's the exact moment that it will be good to try to identify.

If I had not let fear of losing my job and visa get in the way of taking action and adjusting, if I had prioritised my health earlier on after the concussion, I would have probably found another way to deal with it and not have the two and a half years' setback/suffering. I would have had more energy for other good things in work and life and would have enjoyed my first years in Australia more. To take the emotion out of it and look at things more rationally, you need to slow down and invest time to reassess. Don't think you have to stay tough; dare to be vulnerable and ask for help.

Sometimes it's your confidence that's decreasing, your frustration increasing or you're starting to feel physically unwell. Just make sure you give those signs your full attention.

And sometimes, it's about your gut feeling, right? Because we all know analysis paralysis when you're overseeing things. When you catch yourself overthinking things, it's time to take stock and reassess your priorities. If you know and focus where you want to go, it's easier to articulate and take next steps.

USING THE ADVERSITY TO YOUR ADVANTAGE: WHY ADVERSITY STRENGTHENS YOU.

Let me start with the definition of "advantage." In general, it's defined as any state or circumstance or opportunity that's specifically favourable to success or the desired end. In the context of this book, through your insights from adversity, you can be more effective as a leader by building resilience, agility and adaptability. It also makes you appreciate your success more.

For me personally, the true advantage from adversity in both life and business comes when you use the advantage learnings as an *accelerator* to get to your desired outcomes. So, I think that adversity is full of lessons to be learned. Take a step back and analyse or reflect on what has happened. What didn't work well? What can you do better or more effectively next time? How can you see it coming sooner next time? I believe your progress will be faster if you flag the adversity head-on and make faster decisions on it, you'll be more effective than before. This new approach will save you time next time when adversity occurs, as you have 'invested' time in learning while you were experiencing adversity. It will always pay off.

A couple of years ago, one of my coachees was having trouble to free headspace for more strategic work, and trying to be less operational, whilst empowering a team. This is a common theme that I come across.

She was known as a great people manager, but she didn't find the time to be more strategic even though she was already good at delegating.

The adversity she encountered was that her company were losing ground to their competitors and her boss was pressuring her in different ways to apply a more strategic vision and have a better action plan. But he wasn't allowing her more resources. Their working relationship soured somewhat because of it. She knew she had to do something different, apply a new approach to get to the strategic time she needed, improve the relationship and regain the business objectives.

So, she started to reflect where she could delegate and involve her team more and asked them to take broader ownership of projects, which really empowered them. It allowed her to build more trust and gave them new energy. She was able to set new boundaries for herself towards the team, which allowed her to focus more effectively on the bigger picture. From there she was able to drill down to a better action plan, thus securing the business. It also raised her confidence. She had more fun empowering her team as they picked up things quickly; they were happy with more autonomy, and this way her team was better set up for success. She could focus more on her strategic deliverables and setting the direction for the team.

Success doesn't happen overnight. This was no exception. I usually work for about six to nine months with my coaches. I think in this case after three months we had the first shift.

Would you like adversity to strengthen you rather than to weaken you? Because in the VUCA world we live in (VUCA stands for: Volatile, Uncertain, Complex and Ambiguous) there's a lot we need to adapt to as leaders to keep on our toes. It's a complex world we live in. You can't afford to just stay in your comfort zone. You need to keep evolving as a leader to stay relevant and agile to changing conditions around you due to digital disruption and AI. There are no precedents when adversity in our era comes up. You can't always lean on your old experience or approach. Most of the time, you have to find new approaches to deal with new situations. And having had some adversity then definitely could be an advantage as it pushes us out of our comfort zone and we find ways to adapt easier. If you keep your head cool and take time to figure out a new approach, you will be better placed for success.

We don't always like to take a new approach because we would rather stay in our comfort mode. That's just how our brains work. The SCARF model of behaviour, first published by David Rock in 2008, describes it really well through an article on cleverism.com in 2016: "The basic premise of the SCARF model is the assumption the brain makes us behave in certain ways, which are to minimise threats and maximise rewards." Adversity is perceived as a threat at first. Yet the cost of not using adversity to your advantage can be huge. Cost in terms of physical and non-physical health issues. Like headaches, sleep deprivation, procrastination, less time spent on exercise because you're too busy, working more hours yet going around in circles. Not addressing the issue is counterproductive.

You miss out on new learning and insights about how to do things better and your progress will be delayed. There are many reasons why preventing this situation would be better than allowing fear of failure to prevent us dealing with adversity. Let me remind you, successful people don't get there by themselves, it's always a team effort. So, don't be so hard on yourself. If you're stuck in your thoughts for a different approach, reach out and brainstorm together or find a coach or mentor. If we dare to be more vulnerable as a leader and reach out for help/support, people start to think for themselves more and contribute to the team effort.

A great quote from Brene Brown, who is well known for writing about courage and vulnerability in leadership, is: "You can choose courage or you can choose comfort, but you can't have both." I would encourage you to choose courage.

The well-known Harry Potter writer, J.K Rowling, is a great example of using adversity to her advantage. In his article on Inc. about female founders, Jeff Haden described how she stopped pretending to herself to be anything other than what she was and began to direct all her energy to finishing the only work that mattered to her. She was poor as someone in Britain can be without being homeless, as she puts it. Success didn't come to her because of her talent, nor was her every vision clear, or every plan perfect, or every step executed flawlessly. Success was never assured. It was her hard work, perseverance and taking a chance on herself, that turned her adversity to her advantage. It was her growth mindset, her willingness to try. She sent her first novel to 12 publishers and received twelve rejections, only for the thirteenth to publish it. The rest is history.

High performing and successful leaders want to reach their goal more than they fear to fail. And it's why they prioritise the importance of recognising adversity and take action head-on. Because if you wait too long, the issue might get too big. Your ignorance or your fear of failure will grow bigger and it could paralyse you in action.

Another quote that I like is: "It's not the strongest of species that survive nor the most intelligent, but the ones most responsive to change." That's from Charles Darwin. You find out the best approach as you go, while you minimise the damage to your business results or objectives.

No one goes without facing adversity, so it's good to be prepared and have tools to deal with it. You can imagine that resistance to adversity or change will undermine your success and potential for greatness at some point. Your mindset regarding the change often determines how you deal with adversity. Both change and adversity require your action to turn it to your advantage. It's so important to have a growth mindset, and not take change as a threat. Carol Dweck is well known for her work on the mindset psychological trait: Fixed vs Growth mindset. The growth mindset model indicates that having an open mindset and being open for learning and new approaches helps you to be more effective, especially in dealing with adversity. We all know the imposter syndrome that might pop up as well, or fear of loss, or fear of losing the comfort of the status quo that you know so well.

But as a leader, you have to challenge your own thinking and beliefs on loss aversion. What excuse do you give yourself? Keep asking yourself to change your mindset to growth and be open for other options or approaches. Try and keep a growth mindset as a leader. It takes some convincing of self and its why awareness of strengths and values is so important. Knowing which strengths you could use more, and which values are important to you will often point you in the right direction for action and will push you through the adversity. You can read more about strengths in Chapter 6. If you care about your health and fulfilment in your job, make sure you know the tipping point of when enough is enough.

There's always a solution when adversity comes up, always a silver lining. It will usually be an advantage for the future, as long as you are prepared to reflect and see what you could learn to help you next time.

It sounds too easy to say, "have a growth mindset." But if you remind yourself to keep exploring and applying new approaches, and stay willing to practice, and to fine-tune continuously for most effective outcomes, you are on your way. Think back to the elite athletes and famous writers and businesspeople I mentioned earlier; they do that all the time.

Be willing to go out of your comfort zone, actively be open to change. Be willing to accept that failure is an option but know it will lead to more resilience in growth and progress.

Loss aversion, the shame of being stuck or the idea that you're under-performing temporarily is normal. Remind yourself and others we're only human. No one is perfect all the time. Accepting the status quo as your reality will not help you. But realising that the status quo doesn't work for you will help you. So, whenever you find yourself in that position, it's important to ask for help because no one can do it all alone.

WHAT ARE THE ADVERSITY ADVANTAGES?

Let me get right into it. The typical advantages are that you are strengthening your skills and techniques to deal with adversity now and in the future, flagging and preventing it faster. You'll get more effective in dealing with adversity and coming up with new, better approaches. More precisely the advantages can be:

- Increased adaptability, resilience and agility
- Faster and more effective decision making
- Better boundary setting
- Accelerated learning
- Better positioning, getting buy-in and realising inclusion
- Making significant impact
- Anticipating best outcomes
- Increased creativity and productivity
- More head space for strategy, purpose, vision
- Better delegation, empowering and developing a team
- Building confidence in problem-solving and feeling empowered
- Time gained and no further loss of time

Sounds good? If you can't imagine how adversity could benefit you and your team or your business and have no inspiration how it could look, it's hard to get creative and set steps towards the desired business objectives. And with this, focus is of the essence. We all know the saying, "energy flows where focus goes." This is especially true in this VUCA world. We need to be highly adaptable to change, to remain relevant and competitive and effective as a leader.

Sometimes the advantage is the answer to the question: What would you like instead? And some leaders might say: "I wish it would be different." If they can articulate for themselves how "different" would look, they are already half way to finding next steps.

But for sure if you keep doing the same thing, you keep getting the same outcomes. Another one-liner I use is: The same input, doesn't change the output. So, if you would like a different response from a challenging, difficult conversation, you need to change tactics.

As an example, a coachee I worked with was having trouble getting buy-in from the leadership team for his project, and for the new resources he needed. His CEO chairing the meeting didn't champion his points well, and so the leadership team he was part of wasn't aware of all the benefits for the business and rejected his idea. This was true adversity for him as his strategic plan depended on the project's success. He believed in the project and had done lots of research with his team to validate possible success. So, he was willing to try another approach. His fear was of being rejected again and making a fool of himself for raising it again, and he was mindful that he could undermine his CEO. He hadn't prepared the CEO well enough to champion his ideas and didn't speak to any of his fellow leadership team members before the meeting to plant a seed and see what arguments he might need to prepare for. When he did so for the next meeting, we had prepared the right tone and arguments to get his project approved, which resulted in the team adding even more ideas to the topic, which in turn created a richer outcome. My coachee came back stronger and the first thing he said was: "Next time I will take more time to anticipate and prepare and not let fear get in the way and waste precious time." He felt more confident and was happy to have extended his toolbox.

To revisit our metaphor, when the wind changes, you need a sail change. You want to set course again to get to your desired destination. You don't really want that adversity. But if you encounter it, and if you think about its benefits, it helps to respond more quickly. So, you might be thinking, look, the last thing I want is adversity in my life. But if you can shift your perspective so you see the benefit, you'll respond faster and you're likely to get a better outcome.

You always have a choice to change your approach. There was, of course, a chance the leadership team wasn't open to discussing it again, or that other circumstances would arise, but instead of cringing away from the adversity, he actually responded to the challenge and it made him more confident, more constructive.

Always have a growth mindset and be curious. Keep imagining how success could look, even in the face of adversity. As we just saw from the example, in this case, all was not lost after a first try/failure. Create another opportunity by preparing better. The more you increase your adaptability, the more creative and productive you will get, which usually results in faster flagging of adversity and faster addressing it, faster decision making in the near future. Keep evolving and keep taking notes of the learnings. That way you will experience the benefits as a reward.

Remind yourself to tap into your strengths for creativity. What can you do more, or less, of? What seems common is that people get overwhelmed by information overload or they analyse too much. Sometimes small steps are better. (Like the Kaizen theory: Kaizen is the Japanese word for "improvement." Kaizen is an approach to create continuous improvement, based on the idea that small, ongoing positive changes can reap major improvements.) It's better to do *something* about it than nothing. So better to finetune than make no progress at all. Subtle changes do make a difference. And it will also make you feel better and more confident that you will get there.

THRIVING OR SURVIVING? ONLY ACCEPT THE STATUS QUO THAT'S RIGHT FOR YOU

It's no fun as a leader, to 'suffer' through your workday or workweek. Some leaders will argue to just put their head down and work hard to get results. My question for you is: wouldn't it be great if you could look forward to your next working day with anticipation and excitement rather than with dread and apprehension for what might be thrown at you this time?

Let me explain what I think is 'thriving' and what is 'surviving' in a business context.

Thriving at work to me is when you're happy at work, and looking forward to dealing with challenges, change or adversity. You are not afraid, but keen to try out new approaches because you know from former failure how to be more effective, how to keep learning and evolving. You're having fun and fulfilment while role modelling the right behaviours to your team and peers: it's contagious. You're having just the right amount of stress, your input becomes more effortless and you are in flow state, or peak performance. See more on peak performance in Chapter 4.

Surviving looks more like a "have to," dreading your work and the challenges thrown at you. You're trying to keep your head down, ignoring all the signs that things are not working well. You try to postpone taking action, but this is counterproductive. Stress levels are rising and the pressure is on. You're resetting your priorities and deadlines regularly which start to weigh heavy. And you're not very productive or effective, which people will notice. You're procrastinating at night at home and are sleep deprived. Wouldn't you like to do something about it?

The cost of surviving is high. Too high. Work is the biggest part of our daily lives. And how often do we hear about burnouts? It's more common than ever. It's something that's slow-burning and creeping in on someone. And especially people who like to do the best they can, are prone to exhaust themselves to keep up with the workload and pressures. They don't just do it to do well for themselves, but also to please others, to establish a sense of belonging, to keep up their reputation for high performance or to make sure their team is set up for success. It's not all about making long hours, but also, the mental pressure people put on themselves and don't attend to.

Mindfulness, Yoga, meditation or taking a break seem too much work at that time of pressure and are usually prioritised last. But once you reach the burnout phase, it's not just a couple days that you need to recover. It could take well over a year to feel like your old self or the better-recharged version of you. Other costs could be, if this wasn't enough already, not getting the promotion, because your way of working doesn't give your boss the confidence that you can handle more. Anxiety or depression are also very common. And it's hard to keep up any good quality, social life next to that, or hobbies and time outdoors. Is it all worth the effort? Personally, I don't think so.

Another example of surviving I have illustrates when leaders forget how to thrive, and sometimes go on autopilot. And I don't need to tell you, that's not thriving. The leader in question I was working with (a director in a leadership team) wasn't enjoying his role much anymore but it was his way of coping with the demands of the challenging role. Their organisation, market conditions, and role had changed significantly: from a downsizing situation, in which he had been a change manager for years, having had to restructure and let people go, this person had to adapt to being a people manager for their team and drive the growth of their business. However tough this guy seemed, he had only learned to deal with the downsizing pressures, by being very direct and taking no prisoners. Now he needed to negotiate more with peers from the leadership team, to make sure his priorities were being dealt with. He had to change his limiting beliefs (that he couldn't change) and he had to adapt his language. Where he used to say: "It's this way," he didn't leave any room for discussion. This approach had worked for a couple of years quite effectively.

But now there were different times that called for more synergy between the functional areas. When we first started to work, he was not interested in changing his ways and was resistant. After a while, he was willing to try another approach, where he would state his opinion and then add: "what do you think?" his peers responded with surprise at first, but soon responded well by providing him feedback and having a constructive discussion. This is where the synergy started to flourish. My coachee really appreciated it, having more information to make decisions. He also enjoyed learning very quickly how to address his people management issues and drive his business for growth. He didn't feel isolated anymore and enjoyed being part of the leadership team. His confidence grew and he became one of the best managers known for his empowerment of his team. Needless to say, he found his peak performance in this new market situation and thrived again.

Sometimes you can achieve incredible change from a relatively simple strategy. It did take us some time though, as behavioural change addressing limited beliefs and patterns of habit doesn't happen overnight. Sometimes it can take a while, but I always feel it's worth the work. It took some time to get there because we're often in a habit of just fighting adversity, instead of using it to your advantage.

Have a positive mindset. Next to having a growth mindset, leaders with a positive mindset tend to be more creative with their decision making. A can-do attitude and thinking in opportunities and possibilities will smooth the way much quicker, than someone who always sees problems and hurdles. Think about it. It's easier to come up with next steps when you think of what you want or need, then when you think of what you don't want or what you don't need. Nobody is thinking positively all the time, and certainly not in the face of adversity, but it's how you reset yourself and deal with it that makes all the difference.

An example I like to share with you is the story of Tony Robbins I saw on Goalcast. Although his family didn't have much money to spend when he was growing up, he was taught to give instead of take. Tony would give his food to someone else who seemed to need it more. As a kid, he read about 100 books a year and was very keen and determined to become more and more resourceful to make a difference and help/motivate people to do better. His attitude was that through resilience and compassion, you can conquer adversity, and come out stronger. He definitely did so himself. He has become highly successful and is still donating millions of dollars to charity to feed homeless people. His adversity has been a huge driver for him, and he still adheres by giving. I'm a big believer in staying true to yourself and pursuing what it is you need to do in life, and not what you need to avoid.

As you will know by now, my motto in coaching is: "Only accept the status quo that's right for you." In business, it's about leadership effectiveness for a leader to be successful. When someone is not thriving but surviving, they're accepting a status quo that's not right for them. It doesn't serve them to be in a situation where they are facing adversity, but they are not taking enough, or not the right action. So how can you take action on this topic?

First of all, take a step back and reflect. Remind yourself of the bigger picture and what matters to you. And ask yourself for example:

- What were you trying to achieve, before adversity came up?
- What was the direction you were heading?
- Is that still valid or do you need to adjust and adapt that course?
- Identify what thriving is to you and how that would look if you would progress now in the newly adjusted course?
- And what does surviving look like?
- How can you bridge that gap towards thriving?
- What strengths can you tap into to do more or less of and what do you need to let go?
- What limiting thoughts or beliefs are in the way?
- Who can you ask for help, inspiration or advice?
- How can you include and involve your team to problem solve and what can you delegate more to your team?

If you ask yourself these types of questions, you will probably come up with some new insights and thoughts to get started. Even successful people don't thrive on their own. They are really good at acknowledging their strengths, and they know who to reach out to for what, as they have already built a whole toolbox for that, due to their earlier adversity or failures.

When you think about thriving, you might come up against feelings of unworthiness or you might wonder if you deserve to thrive. Self-doubt, imposter syndrome, lack of confidence, lack of strategic insights or approach, all of these are common themes that every leader will experience at some point or even regularly. Reflect for a moment: what got you here? Surely you realise that what got you here, won't get you there (as also explained in Marshall Goldsmith's great book on leadership). But I hope you will also realise on reflection, that "what got you here" means that you already have been evolving into this current leadership role. So, chances are, you can do more evolving and come up with a new approach. You might be in a transition phase or come across a lot of adversity or change, but break that down in small topics and address each of them at a time. Think about the Kaizen theory.

YOU HAVE MORE CHOICE AND CONTROL FACING ADVERSITY THAN YOU MIGHT THINK

One of the most explicit examples on choosing your response I can give you is Victor Frankl's book: *Man's Search for Meaning*. It is an extreme example as it deals with far more challenging circumstances than we usually face in business, but the book inspired me to take learning from Frankl's approach to adversity, which I like to share with you. Sometimes you can't change your circumstances/adversity, but you can always change your response. I would have liked to have offered a different source, but in this case Wikipedia describes it really well: "The bestselling book chronicles his experiences as a concentration camp inmate, which led him to discover the importance of finding meaning in all forms of existence, even the most brutal ones, and thus, a reason to continue living. Frankl became one of the key figures in existential therapy and a prominent source of inspiration for humanistic psychologists. Frankl believes that people are primarily driven by "striving to find meaning in one's life" and that it is this sense of meaning that enables people to overcome painful experiences. After enduring the suffering in these camps, Frankl concluded that even in the most absurd, painful and dehumanised situation, life has potential meaning and that, therefore even suffering is meaningful."

Now, this is, again, the extreme end of adversity and surviving. But what I would hope you can take from this, as a leader, is the belief that you always have more choice and control over adversity than you might think. It's about knowing or exploring what is meaningful for you. What purpose drives you to face any adversity thrown at you, and in business, be successful in your role, in your leadership?

It always makes me a bit sad if I come across leaders who don't believe they have a choice or that they can change things for themselves or be more effective. Call it limiting self-beliefs, self-doubt, lack of confidence, lack of growth or positive mindset, imposter syndrome, they might not know what to make of 'Frankl's quote. "Life is never made unbearable by circumstances, but only by lack of meaning and purpose." A lot of people are so pressured by their workload and so tunnel-visioned in their mindset, that they have gone off course from their purpose. "They tend to forget that purpose is something we do or something we create—not something we buy, inherit or achieve. Purpose could be any direction in which we're heading with some degree of intention. It's a far-reaching, steady goal, something personally meaningful and self-transcending that, ideally, shows up in our lives every day," as quoted from TEDxTraverseCity Talk, Leah Weiss.

Think of people you admire and trace what you like about them back to your own values. Reflecting on the inspirational qualities of a Desmond Tutu or a Ruth Bader Ginsburg or a Beyoncé will shine a light on ourselves. In the traditional Buddhist metaphor, the person we look up to functions as a mirror for our own best self. Or, closer to home, think about who you admire at work. What is it about this person? Aspirational figures don't have to be perfect; just focus on the qualities you admire. (If you can't think of anyone you admire at work that might tell you something.) Purpose and knowing you have a choice are great drivers. Because you're the expert in your field, you have the creativity to come up with the best route for you to get there. In leadership, you always need to keep finetuning your purpose, like a sculpture that's never done or never perfect. Yet you always can come up with ways to enhance it.

IF YOU CAN IMAGINE IT, YOU CAN ACHIEVE IT

Our imagination is key: if you can imagine it, you can achieve it. I entered the tough Round Britain & Ireland Race with no racing experience, just the will and belief to race/crew/to learn got me through. And I loved the experience.

According to Yale School of Management researcher Amy Wrzesniewski, people who consider their work to be a calling felt their work had a purpose. And they tend to be more satisfied than those who think of their work as "just" a job. Having a calling is not restricted to people in executive positions. For example, Wrzesniewski has interviewed hospital janitors who believed they had a calling—they saw their work as more than cleaning; it was about helping support patients' healing. If something is "worth it" really depends on the person and on the day (see also more in Chapter 4). For some leaders I worked with, it's about a clear financial upside to our work that gives meaning. For others, the meaning is in belonging: work relationships and culture are our reasons for getting out of bed. For some, meaning is found in participating in innovation or serving people in need. For many if not most of us, it's a mix of things. And that's what makes it so personal and meaningful for each individual leader.

Don't let yourself get stuck by just pointing fingers at others or blame others for the situation you're in that doesn't work for you. It's immature and naive to think you have no part in that. Also, it will most likely work as a self-fulfilling prophecy. Nobody can read your mind and know what's best for you. If you can articulate your purpose, even at a high level, you can start with your first steps towards that.

So be bold and take a chance. If Victor Frankl can do it, I don't see any exceptions.

Of course, there are situations sometimes, you can't control much of, like Victor Frankl. But most of the time, especially when it's work related, you always have a choice. Start by responding differently to your 'adversity,' whether it's a situation or a person. Decide for yourself that you will make it lighter. You also have the choice to work on your exit strategy or at finding a new job in or outside the organisation etc. That is a choice too. But to keep going and keep on complaining and suffering, that's not good for anyone.

WHO OR WHAT MIGHT BE IN THE WAY?

Have you ever realised that you might be your own biggest hurdle, if you don't reflect or look for help/inspiration? As mentioned before, your self-limited thoughts ("I can't do it" or "They are all against me") and fixed mindset can be a self-fulfilling prophecy as that will then be what you will focus on. However, the same goes for the opposite: if you start to refocus and maybe reflect with a coach or mentor, and ask them to hold a mirror for more inspiration than you might get on your own, you will notice that there's always a different way to think about something and to respond differently to something or someone.

A couple of years ago, one of my coachees didn't have much of a growth mindset when we set out to work together. She was very open about what was in the way for her and how she would like it to be, yet every different approach we discussed she responded by saying it wouldn't work or that she didn't have the time for it. Next to that, she kept rescheduling our appointments as she said she was too busy. At that time, she didn't see that investing time to reflect and redefine her purpose/bigger picture, would help her. In the second half of our collaboration, when work had become so draining and she felt a high level of anxiety to perform, she finally decided to discuss new approaches to her situation, which centred around her boss, who according to her, didn't like her and didn't understand her and didn't support her. When I asked her what she had done before to address this, she admitted she hadn't done anything other than ignoring it, evade her boss and wishing for better times. So, it wouldn't come as a surprise that we still had a lot of options to try out. Firstly, we discussed what she could start to address and how. One of the things was that she needed to leave the office twice a week to pick up her child, as she wanted more quality family time. When she did address it with her boss and also made a suggestion that she would log in an hour in the evening if needed, it was no problem at all. She just hadn't had the courage before to ask, as she believed she wouldn't get the opportunity. A limiting belief and a self-fulfilling prophecy. This was a simple first approach but many more followed. The benefits were that their relationship and mutual understanding improved enormously and she has since been promoted and has developed a well-defined purpose for herself and her team.

CHAPTER CONCLUSION

Do you start to feel empowered by knowing that you can turn your adversity into an advantage? It can strengthen you and it can help you to thrive.

Having more choice and control in leadership—and in life in general— than you might think when facing adversity will increase your leadership adaptability and resilience.

Dare to believe and try out and apply new approaches. Be vulnerable and ask for help. Have a growth mindset and frame positively what it is you like better or want to have more of. Be positive: figure out the 'WHY' and think in 'CAN DO.'

This is just the beginning. Just get started, however small the steps and trust that you have accumulated so much experience from former adversity that you will always find a way.

In the next chapter I will introduce my signature tool, The Scenario Thinking Framework™, to help you with a more specific and pragmatic tool.

INTRODUCING THE SCENARIO THINKING FRAMEWORK™

WHAT IS THE SCENARIO THINKING FRAMEWORK™?

I am about to introduce you to my signature framework called the Scenario Thinking Framework™. It will change the way you think and lead, and increase your leadership adaptability. This framework will help you accelerate your ability to deal with challenges that are clear to you, but which you don't know HOW to approach in the most effective way for best outcomes. By framework, I mean a structured process that allows you to anticipate, prepare and act on next steps in order to quickly get on top of a problematic situation (adversity) and turn it into your advantage. I developed this framework to help myself out of adverse circumstances and. Over many decades, I have finetuned the process, and shown my coachees how to use it and discovered its power.

Mastery of The Scenario Thinking Framework™, that I will explain next, would benefit you if:

- You prefer to thrive instead of to survive
- You want to know how to be on top of your game
- You want to know how to get to where you want to be
- You want to accelerate your personal & professional growth, be the best you can be in the most effective way, but you don't know how exactly
- You are about to have a difficult conversation, but you don't know how
- You need to create buy-in from your peers but you don't know how
- You are expected to always have the overview, but you don't know how
- You need to position yourself for the next level, but you don't know how
- You need to position yourself in your new leadership team, and with stakeholders, but how
- You would like to speak up and share your opinion more, but you don't know how
- You like to be more proactive and anticipatory, but you don't know how
- You like to be more strategic and delegate more, but you don't know how

Once you know how to use the framework—and I am going to show you step-by-step how to use it in this chapter—you will learn to structure your thoughts within a couple of minutes and make more educated and effective decisions, remaining true to yourself. I am sure you know that horrible, sinking feeling you get when you are put on the spot, and you can't think what to say or do. Later, you replay the scenario in your mind, going over all the intelligent responses or decisive actions that come to mind too late. The Scenario Thinking Framework™ will help you to remain calm and come up with a response or next steps that will suit your personality and approach best. It saves precious time in your day. It accelerates your ability to recognise assumptions, limited beliefs, habits or repeating situations and to explore new approaches. Using it builds your confidence and resilience, your creativity and your decision-making. Once you take it on board, you won't get stuck not knowing what to say and do. And, as a result, you spend more time in peak performance mode, and less time struggling, and being frustrated to not achieve best outcomes as you didn't prepare for the situation. Which is not peak performance, right?

CASE STUDY: A TENSE TRANSITION

A coachee I worked with a couple of years ago had had a great career as the director of "Company A." When we met, he had recently moved to "Company B."

Company B had a whole different culture. My coachee was new to Company B's way of working, set of values and organisational structure. As his transition coach, my job was to accelerate his adaptability so he could make some changes in the organisation and for his team, fast.

He was already a couple weeks into the job when we started to work together, and we had to do a little bit of damage control. He had set up a lot of meetings to position himself in his new leadership team, but his approach and way of working didn't go down well in the new company. People responded to him with some resistance. He lost confidence and, to regain a little sanity, he got stuck into the operational side of his role. This was his comfort zone, and he quickly retreated into it and avoided the strategic and leadership parts of his job. But leading the operations was only a small part of what he was paid for. He had to adapt so he could step outside his comfort zone and get back to leadership.

HAVE YOUR REALITY CHECK WITH THE SCENARIO THINKING FRAMEWORK™

My job was to challenge my coachee to articulate his current unwanted situation, and after that, his ideal solution to the problems he faced. This is among the first steps in using the Scenario Thinking Framework™. (There are a couple of steps that come before, which I will outline shortly.) He told me that for him, in general terms, this ideal solution was a workplace where he didn't have any resistance and felt a strong synergy with his new colleagues.

We started with his situation as it stood. My coachee needed to see and feel the considerable gap between where he was currently and where he wanted to be. That is a critical element of using the framework: having a reality check about the problem. Most of my coachees are solution-focused. As soon as they identify a problem, they want to solve it. But to use the Scenario Thinking Framework™, you first need to see that you don't like where you are, or that it doesn't work for you, and that your old approach doesn't serve you anymore. So together, we first articulated what the current, unwanted situation was. Then we explored and articulated in detail how unresolved his situation was and the frustration he felt being in that situation.

THE SCENARIO THINKING FRAMEWORK™ HELPS YOU TO ANTICIPATE, PREPARE AND ACTION NEXT STEPS, INCREASING YOUR LEADERSHIP ADAPTABILITY

This process is aimed at leaders who are or have been mostly successful already, with a high level of performance, but who have become stuck or feel like they're stagnating on specific topics. Nobody is successful all the time. People have situations they're less adapted to, or they have temporarily lost their positive outlook or energy. But successful people are driven to be the best they can be, and they are in these leadership roles because they have succeeded and accomplished a great deal. The more senior you get, the more complex your world will be. At the top level, the role is about soft skills, influencing, negotiation, positioning, and leading others. You have a lot of situations thrown at you, and it will be hard to prioritise and deal effectively with all of them at the same time. Time pressures and constant change can undermine your confidence and problem-solving skills. This process assumes that you have experienced adversity before and that you like to come out stronger and better each time you face it.

HOW THE SCENARIO THINKING FRAMEWORK™ DIFFERS FROM OTHER FRAMEWORKS

The Scenario Thinking Framework™ is about thinking through and articulating the ideal outcomes and moving away from a current, unwanted situation. The difference between this and other frameworks (like design thinking or strategic planning) is that this is a leadership tool. It helps you first, and then you can help your business. It's like the air-safety instructions: put your own mask on first, and then help others.

Frameworks like design thinking or strategic planning are business tools. Scenario planning or strategic planning helps organisations to make flexible, long-term plans. They are adaptations of classic methods used by military intelligence. Design thinking is more relevant to the innovation of new products or resources and refers to the cognitive, strategic, and principle processes by which design concepts are developed by designers or design teams.

BEFORE YOU START USING THE SCENARIO THINKING FRAMEWORK™

Those two steps I took my coachee through come early in the Scenario Thinking Framework™ –and I'll explain the rest shortly. But I want to add something important here: you can't use the Scenario Thinking Framework™ effectively until you put into action all the other elements that I raise in this book. The Scenario Thinking Framework™ is the central tool, and it will always help you to find clarity on next steps. But it won't rock your world and change the way you think unless you do all the work in the other chapters of this book. You must learn to:

- Understand the difference between being a high achiever and a high performer
- Recognise and be self-aware of your own DNA make up and peak performance
- Reset and find the overview
- Manage your strengths and recognise when you over use or under use them
- Use my suggested neuroscience hacks that will set you up for success and make it all much more effortless

After my coachee felt the reality of the unwanted situation he was in, I challenged him with questions about his strengths, beliefs and behaviours—the topics addressed in later chapters. I coached him through the tools mentioned in this book. It was after he had dealt with each of these challenges that he came up with a new approach. That allowed him to complete the remaining steps in the Scenario Thinking Framework™, position himself better as a leader and improve his communication skills.

USING THE SCENARIO THINKING FRAMEWORK™ AS YOUR SUPER TOOL

I left home young; I was still finishing high school. As a high achiever, I felt driven by a need for freedom and independence. Leaving home challenged me in dealing with adversity. I had to provide for myself financially and keep myself out of trouble. I had to make impactful decisions and set my own course. My motto, from that time onward, has always been: "Only accept the status quo that's right for you." By this I mean that if the situation you find yourself in is not right for you, whatever the reason, do something about it. Don't dwell in it. Pursue a better status quo, one that's right for you. Make sure your conditions make you happy.

Of course, just like everyone, my challenges didn't stop when I grew older; many more were to follow. When I moved to Australia, I was 44 years old and I had a dream of setting up my own business again (I'd already run a business in my home country of Holland) and building a new life. I had to take many steps and overcome some considerable hurdles. The Scenario Thinking Framework™ helped me in the challenging situation of permanently moving countries to think in a structured and strategic way to achieve my desired outcomes.

As I have outlined earlier in this book, I have had several concussions (luckily no permanent damage). While overcoming my most severe concussion, I had regular panic attacks because I was anxious that I would not pull it off and recover fully. I'd used the Scenario Thinking Framework™ many times to stop the pressure getting to me, and to regain creativity and productiveness when I was out of inspiration. Today, in my coaching business, after some 25-plus years of experience, I have stayed true to this motto. I love helping others to thrive in a situation, or to succeed in the position they are in: Accelerating their leadership effectiveness, using the Scenario Thinking Framework™ as their super tool. When I share my earlier adversity with my coachees, they quickly see many parallels with the challenges they face as leaders in their businesses.

WHEN TO USE THE SCENARIO THINKING FRAMEWORK™

Whenever you encounter any kind of adversity in business—a new status quo that doesn't work for you—use this framework. For some problems, action is the only change agent, but you must have a plan to navigate it; adversity doesn't solve itself. If you keep doing the same thing, you keep getting the same outcomes. In every chapter of this book, I'll reveal situations in which you can use the framework to make essential changes in the way you operate as a leader.

If you are in a leadership role using the framework regularly, you have a way of thinking fast, making solid decisions and preparing well for meetings. It's your secret superpower and will increase your confidence to easily deal with any situation thrown at you.

And if you don't innovate as a leader, you will not progress or be a good role model for your team. Companies have never needed leadership more than they do now in a world where disruption is continuous. Leaders must be agile, adaptable and resilient; they must be fast thinking, quick decision-makers.

According to the World Economic Forum, the most transferable skills in the future include complex problem solving, critical thinking, creativity and people management. The framework helps you to do all of those and move into your peak performance, where you are at your best and working most productively. I will elaborate further on peak performance in Chapter 4.

HOW TO USE THE SCENARIO THINKING FRAMEWORK™

The Scenario Thinking Framework™ is a way to get from A to B. It is that simple. That is why I use the symbol of the arrow to get my coachees started, to point them in the right direction. The arrow begins where you are finding yourself, in the current or unwanted situation. The situation that doesn't work for you anymore. And the arrow goes to your ideal situation, where you experience best outcomes for yourself and the people around you that are involved. The more you practice drawing the arrow and using the process around it, the better you will get at anticipating, preparing and taking next steps, achieving best outcomes. It requires practice.

PRE REQUISITE: KNOW YOURSELF AND INCREASE YOUR SELF-AWARENESS

As I mentioned earlier, you have to do the work, meaning get regular feedback or a 360 degrees assessment on how you behave in the workplace, how you are performing and how you are perceived, before you use the Scenario Thinking Framework™, because it is going to throw up a variety of challenges. Self-awareness of your DNA make up is key, to know what works best for you, which buttons to push (what to do more or less of) and how to remain true to yourself.

STEP 1: DRAW THE ARROW

We are going to start by drawing an arrow, horizontally on a blank page, from left to right. Nice and long, please, so that you can add your thoughts to it. How simple is that?

STEP 2: EXPLORE, UNPACK AND ARTICULATE YOUR UNWANTED SITUATION

If you, like me, are a high achiever, this step is harder than you might think. Like my coachee in Company B, you probably think of solutions to problems so fast you barely even notice you have a problem. Slow down, take a deep breath and reflect. What keeps you up at night? You must know you find yourself in an unwanted situation that you like to resolve, before you start using the Scenario Thinking Framework™. When you start, think of two or three best outcomes. Don't try to solve everything at once. Give yourself a reality check. It looks look this:

1. Draw the arrow:

2. Describe current unwanted situation:

- My approach, way of working doesn't seem to work
- I feel resistance from peers
- Lost confidence, frustrated
- I'm stuck in operational/comfort zone
- I need to adapt/step up
- I need to show leadership, strategic vision

3. Describe ideal situation/best outcomes:

- Workplace with constructive working relationships
- Synergy with peers, progressing on projects
- Confidence up, clear headspace for strategic vision
- Peers invite me more for strategic catch ups
- Peers come to me for advice/synergy

As shown in the Scenario Thinking Framework™ on page 43

THE SCENARIO THINKING FRAMEWORK™

A reality check & best outcomes regarding the Case study: A tense transition:

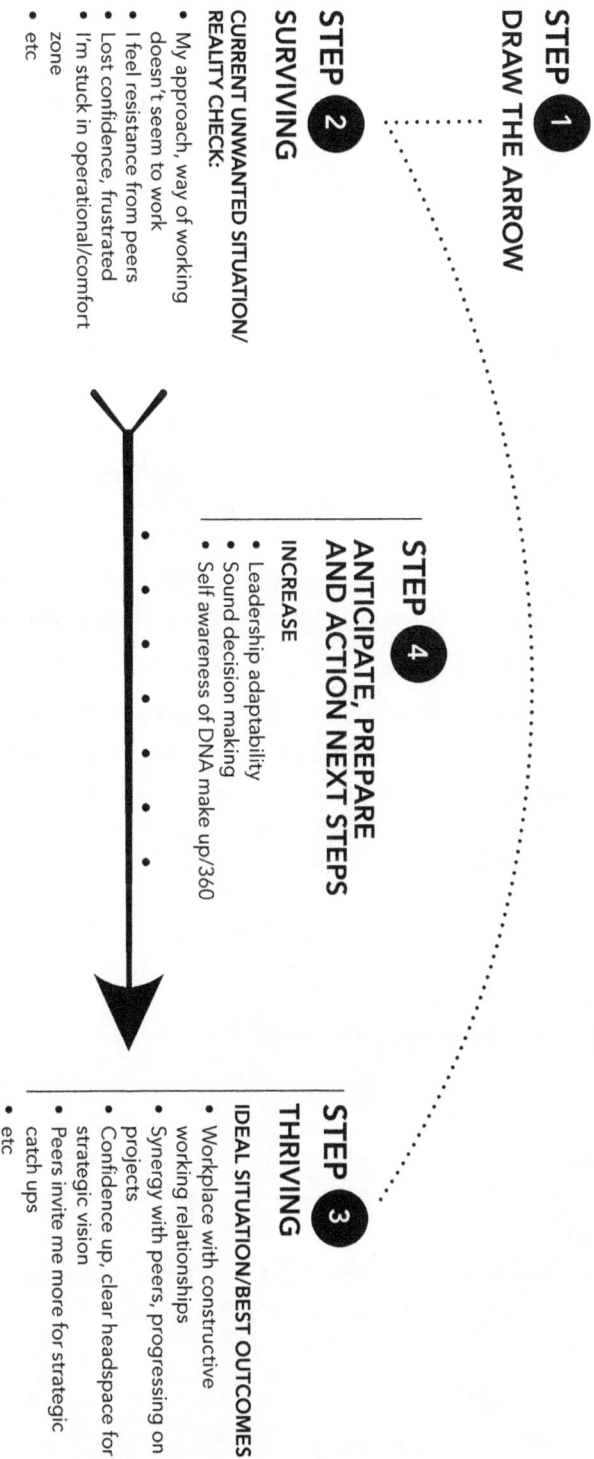

STEP 1
DRAW THE ARROW

STEP 2
SURVIVING

**CURRENT UNWANTED SITUATION/
REALITY CHECK:**

- My approach, way of working doesn't seem to work
- I feel resistance from peers
- Lost confidence, frustrated
- I'm stuck in operational/comfort zone
- etc

STEP 4
ANTICIPATE, PREPARE AND ACTION NEXT STEPS

INCREASE

- Leadership adaptability
- Sound decision making
- Self awareness of DNA make up/360

STEP 3
THRIVING

IDEAL SITUATION/BEST OUTCOMES

- Workplace with constructive working relationships
- Synergy with peers, progressing on projects
- Confidence up, clear headspace for strategic vision
- Peers invite me more for strategic catch ups
- etc

On the left-hand side of the arrow, step 2, is your current, unwanted situation. Here you'll make your top-of-mind quick-thinking notes about the situation that doesn't work for you, using exact keywords. And remember, we are not talking about long-term strategies or planning here, we are talking about specific situations, like a difficult working relationship with a peer you would like to improve, a challenging meeting or a problematic conversation that is coming up etc.

Now is the time to explore and unpack the unwanted situation and go as deeply into that as you will do so later (step 3), with your ideal outcome, which will be at the right-hand side of the arrow. Why must you be so detailed in your approach? If you don't focus on the detail, it's not clear what the hurdles are. Without clarity, it's difficult to come up with a solution or approach. Sometimes, using the Scenario Thinking Framework™ is the first time that you really articulate the problem; you haven't thought in depth about your situation before, or articulated the feelings of frustration you experience, for yourself.

None of us wants to change their approach unless the pain of the situation we are in (adversity) is more than we can stand or accept. And high achievers have a high pain threshold. So, this step is essential. Often, my coachees try to move past this one, but I take them back into it again. I want them to discover their intrinsic motivation to change.

For example, your current, unwanted situation could be: "I must have buy-in at the next meeting, but I don't know how right now, or how to influence and it makes me anxious. But without the buy-in, I probably don't get a green light for my project."

Your keywords for step 2, on the left of the arrow could be:

- Need green light but can't get buy-in. Anxious. Fear of failing again
- Getting the cold shoulder from my peers at a personal level. Lonely
- Resistance: Team members and peers saying "no" to my ideas. Frustrated
- Powerless: Team missing deadlines I set, which causes new problems

STEP 3:
IMAGINE AND ARTICULATE
YOUR BEST OUTCOMES

How can you get to your best outcomes if you don't know what they look like or how to describe them? You must ask yourself: What is the ideal situation you are striving for? Like my coachee described in the example above. Imagine and articulate those best outcomes. Without knowing your best outcomes and how to articulate them, it will be hard to get there. You might, but it would be unlikely. Use your notebook to write down your ideal solution to your problem to the right of the arrow. Unpack that ideal outcome and articulate in detail. How would it feel, sound or look being in your ideal situation, and what would it allow you? Use specific keywords, describe your ideal outcomes and how that will improve your situation. For example, if the issue is the buy-in, how will it feel if you get it—relieved, happy, empowered—and what precisely will that be like—I will get support, I can take these next steps, I have more information and feedback than I thought. Then describe what it will allow you and your team to do—my group is engaged and gets more creative, thinking on their feet, cutting some red tape, for example.

Now summarise that ideal into a few key words as step 3 and write it at the right of the arrow. It might be:

- Buy-in at my next meeting. Happy, relieved. Team creative and productive
- A warm response to my leadership. Collegial, relaxed
- A 'yes' to my proposal. Effective and empowered
- My team member is meeting the deadline I set. Respected

STEP 4:
ASK YOURSELF WHAT YOU MUST DO TO
GET FROM YOUR CURRENT, UNWANTED
SITUATION TO YOUR IDEAL OUTCOMES

Now, using the length of the arrow as a timeline, write down the first thing that comes to mind as a next step, even if it seems foolish once it is out of your head. Write down next steps, before the space where you have written down the ideal outcomes at the pointy end. Next steps might be:

- Convince yourself you must improve your current situation for better outcomes
- Delegate more to your team with their development goals in mind
- Check in with a trusted peer, how they dealt with a similar situation
- Set up a team meeting to ensure they have the tools to contribute to the bigger picture
- Ask for more information from a peer or specific department

STEP 5:
CHALLENGE YOURSELF EVEN MORE
WITH HARD QUESTIONS

Again, using the length of the arrow as a timeline, you ask yourself another series of questions to find out what you can do, what next steps you can take, how you can address the obstacles in your way, and what information you still need. This is not about figuring out how another person thinks; this is about reflecting on yourself and what you can do more or better as an approach. Think of real-life examples about that situation, how it shows up, when it shows up, how it makes you feel, and what happens. How do you usually respond? For example, you could say that you don't know what your leadership team really thinks about the idea that they are resisting. Your reaction to recognising you don't know what they think will tell you about your mental state around this situation. For instance, you may realise you acted without thinking because you felt threatened. Then you encountered some resistance.

Challenge yourself with hard questions and come up with positively framed next steps as answers. If my team member doesn't deliver on time, what could I do to help them or set a better example? If my resistant peer is open for a conversation, how could I influence them to embrace my ideas? For everyone to listen to me, what words must I change? What is the first step I must take to make my team more helpful and productive?

Write down the answers on the timeline according to where you think they might go in a sequence.

STEP 6:
AT EVERY NEXT STEP, CHALLENGE YOURSELF TO INCREASE YOUR COURAGE AND CONFIDENCE

As you write down your answers, challenge yourself with questions about how to make the action happen. Every answer is a next step anticipating and preparing for a different approach to get to your ideal situation. You will have to find out which strengths to use more or less of (see Chapter 6), what values are important to you, and which best practices might help you to find the answers. If you lack self-awareness, it will be hard to figure out by yourself. If you get stuck, ask a coach or trusted colleague or friend for help to find the next question and the next step.

Work towards your next course of action. For example, should you approach a peer and ask for input? Write down the steps that you must do, the information and resources you need to get to your desired outcome. As you go along, you will encounter self-limiting beliefs. Imposter syndrome can also be a big challenge for many people. If you lack the belief that you can achieve your goal, your confidence will take a hit. That is why you reflect and do the work in the other chapters, assessing your strengths (Chapter 6), values and goals together to address what is really important to you. Then you can shift your self-beliefs in a positive direction so that you don't feel like an imposter and believe that you can find a solution for your problems.

Addressing each of these limitations is a next step on the timeline. The types of barriers you encounter will determine your course of action. For example, a next step might be: Enter the meeting with the leadership team in a positive frame of mind. Remind myself that I have a history as an effective leader and will solve this leadership problem. Coming out of that meeting will increase your confidence and you will next time use your courage even more.

THE SCENARIO THINKING FRAMEWORK™

Full flow powered by using:
EMPATHY, FUTURISTIC, ACTIVATOR, MAXIMISER, DISCIPLINE

STEP 1
DRAW THE ARROW

STEP 2
SURVIVING

**CURRENT UNWANTED
SITUATION/ REALITY CHECK:**

Write down keywords to the below
questions to unpack the unwanted
situation:

**DESCRIBE THE SITUATION THAT'S
NOT WORKING FOR YOU:**

- What's the adversity?
- Whats not working specifically?
- Who is involved?
- Whats their behaviour you struggle with?
- What behaviour are you displaying?
- Describe what you struggle with or find
  challenging in this situation?
- When does this needs to be solved/
  solution found?
- What are you feeling atm: Stuck?
  Surviving? Autopilot? Head down,
  Pushing through? Ignoring? Given up?
- What are the hurdles?
- From whom do you need support
  or buy in?
- What information do you need
  to progress?

STEP 4

**ANTICIPATE, PREPARE
AND ACTION NEXT STEPS:**

What is important to you and
What does this mean to you?

Some questions to remind
yourself:

STEP 5

**CHALLENGE YOURSELF WITH
HARD QUESTIONS!**

Reflect on yourself and what you
can do more or better as an approach:

**WHAT CHOICES DO YOU HAVE
TO RESPOND?**

- How to use the adversity to
  your advantage?
- What do you like to change or
  adapt regarding step/box 2?
- Reset and overview
- Reframing in positive wording
  (I need, I like to, instead of,
  I don't need, or I don't like to)

- STF leads to increased leadership adaptability and decision making
- STF is about determining what's not working for you now and why
- Anticipating on the ideal outcome in short term future
- Activating or preparing next steps to the ideal outcome
- Maximising or actioning next steps to the ideal outcome
- Discipline and persistence to see things through

INCREASE AND ACCELERATE YOUR:
- Leadership adaptability
- Sound decision making
- Self awareness of DNA make up/360

HOW DOES THIS ADVERSITY RELATE TO YOUR:

- Purpose
- Strengths
- Assumptions
- Beliefs
- Behaviour affected
- Values: still intact or compromised?
- Role models
- Business objectives
- Coaching objectives

STEP 6

AT EVERY NEXT STEP, CHALLENGE YOURSELF TO INCREASE YOUR COURAGE AND CONFIDENCE:

As you write down your answers, challenge yourself with questions about *how* to make the action happen. Every answer is a next step.

ASK YOURSELF: WHAT STEPS DO YOU NEED TO PROGRESS?

- Resources?
- Information?
- Buy in?
- Support?
- Endorsement?
- Action - steps?
- Which strengths to use more or less of?
- What values are important to you?
- Which best practices might help you anticipating to and preparing a different approach to get to your ideal situation?

STEP 3

THRIVING

FUTURE IDEAL SITUATION/BEST OUTCOMES:

DESCRIBE HOW YOU WANT IT TO BE

- How would you like (it) to be instead?
- How does the ideal outcome look/feel?
- When will you be happy with the outcome?
- What is the outcome described in detailed keywords?
- What does this outcome allow you?
- How does this outcome help others?
- How does success look like?
- What would be different?

STEP 7:
IMPLEMENT YOUR PLAN OF ACTION

When you finish going through the framework process, you have a plan of action, with clear steps to find your best approach for the unwanted situation, that challenging meeting or problematic conversation. Every answer along the arrow is a next step that will move you from your current, unwanted situation to your ideal situation. You might rearrange a couple of points, add or delete a step, but you will be astonished at how accurate—and how powerful—the plan you have developed with the Scenario Thinking Framework™ will be. It is a road map to achieving better, more effective outcomes whilst increasing your leadership adaptability.

By using this process, you'll clearly see what the gap is between where you are now and where you want to go. And usually, the difference isn't that big. It's usually *you* that might be holding back, by not believing that you can pull it off in a more effective way, and assuming how others will think or respond to your ideas. By addressing one obstacle head-on, you build confidence and can move onto the next step in the progression. It takes practise, but when your confidence grows, you will get more creative. When you take these steps, you'll feel like you're on to something, and it will be easier for you to cross that gap that you've identified.

We're not talking about long-term outcomes here. Every step has more short-term gain in mind, however these will help you find more long-term, sustainable and effective approaches. If the step is something that requires a longer-term goal, you can use the arrow multiple times adding steps, building on progress or starting a new arrow whenever you like to refresh your approach. For example, you may want to shift your team from being task-oriented to thinking on their feet. To do that, you must change the behaviour or empower your team. Changing behaviour usually requires a more consistent, longer-term approach. Take the steps you have laid out on the timeline. Every couple of weeks, reflect on your progress and how it has shifted, and build from there.

WHY THE SCENARIO THINKING FRAMEWORK™ WORKS

CHALLENGE YOUR THINKING

Basically, the steps in the framework challenge your thinking. First, you draw on your gut feeling, the answer that comes to mind as the most authentic. Then the questions you challenge yourself with clarify your thoughts on where you are now and where you'd like to be instead.

KNOW YOUR STRENGTHS

Later, in Chapter 6, I talk about various strength assessment tools, including one by Gallup. When I did the Gallup strength assessments it came out with:

- Empathy
- Futuristic
- Activator
- Maximiser
- Discipline

It probably wouldn't surprise you that the principles of my top five strengths make up for the basic elements of the Scenario Thinking Framework™. When you use the framework, you will draw on strengths such as empathy and your futuristic outlook, and skills as an activator and maximiser to create next steps and to put them in motion, with discipline regarding continuous and consistent practice. You will fine-tune and implement a new approach to achieve your desired outcomes. As a coach, I use my strengths to help you get best outcomes.

REFLECTION IS KEY FOR YOUR PREPARATION

When you draw an arrow horizontally from left to right over the full width of a page on your notebook as the starting element, you visualise time and thought. You reflect when you write your keywords as you anticipate and prepare your next steps for a future event. In essence, the framework is a reflection framework that enhances your thinking, challenges your limited beliefs and your unproductive behaviours using reflection, and defines your action points into keywords. It prepares you to make effective decisions.

BUILD CONFIDENCE

You are always better off preparing for future events. Time is money, as the saying goes. And it is more than money. Time is precious, as having too little of it can affect our health and happiness. It is about looking after yourself and your family and other relationships. Being a capable, well-prepared decision maker is the best use of time, money and your high achieving brain. It benefits every business and every business leader. I know you are already good at what you do, but you haven't experienced yet how much better you could be. My coachees regularly surprise themselves with how good the outcome can be and what they are capable of when using the framework correctly and effortlessly.

GET THE SCENARIO THINKING FRAMEWORK™ INTO YOUR MUSCLE

When I talk about getting the framework "into your muscle," I mean developing a new habit. I mean getting the principle of the framework and the process into your muscle. When it is established as a process in your muscle, it takes minutes or seconds to work through the framework.

Get familiar with it and practice. Without practice, it won't work as effectively. It's like learning a new sport. You won't score a goal if you're running with the ball or shooting a ball for the first time. You must know the rules of the game and how the field is set up, drawing the arrow and taking next steps in the process. You can't expect it to work smoothly from the first go.

When I introduce the framework to my coachees, and we identify their current and ideal situation, I drive the process for them. I draw the arrow and then ask them the questions and guide them through it. This way, they can learn the correct process before they do it themselves. They see how it can play out and how it helps their thinking and decision-making, and they can come up with more alternatives. But keep in mind that the situation is unique for everyone, and so is someone's DNA make up. So, you need to be creative with the questions to ask and tailor it to the individual's situation.

But you don't have to do it this way. If you do everything I have suggested in this chapter, you will quickly improve your thinking and decision-making capacity. The evidence of success for having a growth mindset is demonstrated by elite athletes, formula one drivers or violinists. It always takes practise to get good at something. The benefits depend upon the scenario, but you will save yourself time and heartache by giving yourself the tools to deal with whatever obstacle or adversity that has been thrown at you. Still, we often resist what is good for us and in our best interests. Here are some of the typical barriers.

THE IMPORTANCE OF POSITIVE PSYCHOLOGY AND REFRAMING

When you're working with the framework, positive psychology and positive framing of the way you talk to yourself, describing a situation and the way you speak to others, is vital. Positive psychology is a scientific study of human flourishing and an applied approach to optimal functioning. Mark Setton, D.Phil., and Paul Desan, MD, Ph.D., co-founders of Pursuit of Happiness, explain "that the term "Positive Psychology" was originally coined by the psychologist Abraham Maslow in the 1950s. He used the term somewhat loosely to call for a more balanced view of human nature, that is, to draw attention to human potentialities as well as psychological afflictions. In 2002, Martin Seligman popularised Positive Psychology through his influential work *Authentic Happiness*, defining it as the study of positive emotions and the "strengths that enable individuals and communities to thrive." Positive Psychology is largely focused on the study of positive emotions and "signature strengths." Setton and his team design and teach educational programs on the science and implementation of well-being for academic institutions and corporations such as Google, MediaMax, the China Accelerator, Dartmouth College, etc. They describe the seven habits of happy people: Having close relationships; cultivating acts of kindness; exercising and physical wellbeing; being in flow state (see more in Chapter 4); spiritual engagement and meaning, strengths (Chapter 6) and virtues and a positive mindset: optimism, mindfulness and gratitude (Chapter 7).

When we talk about the framework, and when I ask my coachees what their ideal situation looks like, it all leads back to that. We look at how it contributes to either a fulfilling life or your fulfilment in a role. I believe very much in living your best life and functioning to your full potential in business. Therefore, we must be aware of our strengths, values and purpose to pursue that. Positive thinking and positively framing your thoughts and words are imperative.

It will help you see and create opportunities rather than thinking in obstacles. Problem-solving becomes more natural, your creativity increases, and you will be better at relationship building. As a coach who always has positive psychology in mind, I help to shift the focus from something wrong to the promotion of wellbeing. It's filled with meaning, engagement, positive relationships and accomplishments, so you're building something constructively. It's also designed to assist in lasting, sustainable change.

RESISTANCE #1:
"I'M DOING PERFECTLY WELL, THANK YOU."

You might be thinking you've never used the framework, yet you are high up on the corporate ladder. Of course, the Scenario Thinking Framework™ is not the only framework or approach. But I bet you've addressed the elements of the Scenario Thinking Framework™ in one way or another.

What I would love to do is surprise you with what you're capable of if you followed the complete framework. This model is designed explicitly for overcoming adversity; to increase your adaptability, decision-making and resilience; and to position yourself effectively. I dare every leader to try out the framework.

If there's something that's not going according to plan, that you would like to change, enhance or speed up, you can then use the framework on that. For example, let's say you have a working relationship with a peer that can be improved. You have a meeting with them next week where you need their input on a presentation for the leadership team, but you're not sure if you will get that positive input. Not everyone feels the need or dares to address this, but with the Scenario Thinking Framework™ as your tool, you can address this issue more smoothly than you might think and have a greater chance at success.

You might not believe that it can be done. People say to me, "No, I've tried to prepare many times in the past." But you have not combined all these elements in a structured way. And again, remind yourself to have a growth mindset. Come on, give it a go.

RESISTANCE #2: IS IT FLUFFY?

Many people tell me they believe positive psychology is fluffy. Positive psychologists seek to encourage acceptance of one's past and excitement and optimism about future experiences. Its practitioners attempt psychological interventions that foster positive attitudes towards one's subjective experience. The goal is to minimise any pathological and non-positive thoughts that may result in a hopeless mindset. Instead, we develop a sense of optimism towards life and a growth mindset. In the framework, I focus on figuring out how something can look in the future you want to work towards in detail to build that growth and change mindset. That's not fluffy, but very real.

It's more about tricking your own brain. Elite athletes, when they go to the

Olympics, are tricking their brain into feeling like they're already holding up the trophy and telling themselves how it will feel when they've won. That's an example of visualising the achievement and a very positive mindset. In business, if you have a positive mindset, it works the same way. When you shift to telling yourself that you will get there and what it will look like, you're tricking your brain. That will enhance your clarity of mind and creative thinking, and help you find the resources to get there. Your brain doesn't know the difference between what is real and what isn't.

Notice how you communicate. How often do you say, "I don't want this," "I don't like that," "I don't need this"? And now focus on what you DO want, like, or need. Using negative wording makes it hard to feel positive and solution-focused at the same time, but positive wording will push you in the right direction.

I often work with people who are in their 40s and 50s. They have busy lives, partners, kids and other responsibilities outside work. When they have kids, I encourage them to use positive psychology on their kids first. Kids, especially when they're in puberty, are challenging to communicate with, as we all know. We have been there. The framework helps parents talk with them because it triggers kids to think for themselves. That also builds trust and respect. Sometimes my coachees tell me that they've tried it on their kids or their partners and, because it was successful, they now feel confident to use it on their team as well.

RESISTANCE #3: IT IS HARD WORK OR TAKES UP TOO MUCH TIME

You might be thinking to yourself: this is too long and complicated. But it requires less effort than you might think to use this framework. Yes, the first time you use it, it takes time. But once you know the steps and you practise it a bit, you will have it "in your muscle." Then it will be fast and effortless. You'll fly through it and arrive at solutions faster than you think.

Preparation is vital if you want to be useful as a leader and communicate well. Many leaders go into a meeting or a one-on-one conversation without preparation because we are all under time pressure and managing a big workload. But, in my experience, leaders can be over-confident that they will have a good meeting, even without preparation. They run from one meeting to another, thinking to themselves, "Right, what are we talking about here? What must I achieve here?" They waste precious time in the first few minutes of the meeting getting their bearings.

I get it. We all do it. But in those precious minutes, somebody who's better prepared might set the tone for a particular topic. Once that is done, even the best leader will have a hard time convincing others to look at the issue in a different way. Has that happened for you? It has for me. Suddenly, I feel an increase in pressure because it's not going my way and time is running out. Once we get into this mental state, it's difficult to be creative and improvise an approach that will land your point and influence others on the spot. When human beings experience too much stress, our brains tend to 'freeze' (see more about this in chapter three and four), and we become reactive in our communication. We don't take enough time to think and respond, let alone think creatively. When that happens, you sell yourself and others short.

You will save time and be prepared using the Scenario Thinking Framework™. Even if there's a problem that could be solved with your usual approach, try the Scenario Thinking Framework™ because it is great to practice it on "easy" issues. And you will get more effective and limit possible frustration.

When you master the Scenario Thinking Framework™, it will make you a proactive, effective and fast decision maker. As you structure the way you think through decisions, you communicate them consistently and clearly. Your processes will become more transparent to people you're leading, building trust and role modelling. It's all about increased adaptability by becoming more aware of your intention and how that intention "shows up" in the way you lead. The Scenario Thinking Framework™ allows you to share your positive intentions and purpose and take your staff through your train of thought, because you have explored your own thought process in detail.

The Scenario Thinking Framework™, like every great idea, seems simple. It is a simple principle or process, made complex because of our assumptions, limiting beliefs and habits. For every coachee I have introduced this framework to, it has been a revelation. Of course, when they first encounter it, they say, "I don't have the time to prepare properly" or "Yes, I've thought about it." But they soon discover they haven't included all the elements of the framework and therefore didn't have an effective outcome. As I mentioned, a lot of behavioural insight and awareness of strengths and values sits behind effectively using the framework. Which is why I wrote the other chapters in this book.

CHAPTER CONCLUSION

If you acknowledge adversity as a sign that you can take action and change the status quo, the Scenario Thinking Framework™ is an excellent framework for you. By using it, you can accelerate effective outcomes and learnings and apply them to future events in the shorter term or longer term. But it's an individual process. It's for you to improve your effectiveness as a leader, and to help grow a high-performing team. It's not meant to replace strategic planning or design thinking. It is an adjunct to these organisational strategies. Have a growth mindset and turn adversity into an advantage by using it with curiosity and determination.

In the rest of this book, I will give you all the tools you need to make the Scenario Thinking Framework™ work for you. We start, in the next chapter, by identifying the difference between the high achiever and a high performer. You must be able to tell the difference so that you can use the framework to shift between these two states at will. This way getting into peak performance will be easier to achieve.

SHIFTING FROM HIGH ACHIEVER TO HIGH PERFORMER

The first step to dealing with adversity in the most effective way is to understand the difference between a High Achiever and a High Performer. Why does this matter? Because increased self-awareness is the key to being an effective and authentic leader.

Most people think that the words "High Achiever" and "High Performer" are interchangeable. Did you even know there was a difference? Don't be shy about saying "no." I didn't fully appreciate that either, at first. I never looked into it in much detail, to be honest. I used the words "High Achiever" for both high achiever and high performer. But after a client was kind enough to provide me with feedback on a presentation that I made for them and mentioned that they prefer to work with high performers, I did some research that clarified a lot. I have learned that these two groups are quite different, and I will explain the differences in this chapter.

To start with, one of the biggest differences between high achievers and high performers, especially noteworthy for you as a leader: high performers are often more effective in achieving their goals or objectives, involving others on their journey, and more mature and balanced in their approach, than typical high achievers.

Therefore, it is important to know how to shift from high achiever to high performer when required, so that you can recognise and realise where you're at, which approach you must take to course correct, and how you can lead more effortlessly and more effectively in a sustainable way going forward.

Knowing how to shift will also enable you to accelerate your journey from acting like a manager (telling your team what to do) to truly being a leader (role modelling successful behaviours while empowering your team). If you don't know what the difference is and how to make that shift, you might not be working to your and your team's full potential. You might not get the outcomes you are after or achieve the goals you had set for yourself and your team. Simply said: You won't make the best use of your time.

WHAT DO I MEAN BY HIGH ACHIEVERS?

High achievers, of course, are motivated and driven to achieve. Where less accomplished individuals are often more motivated to avoid failure, high achievers are often very hard on themselves and laser-focused and persistent on the goals they would like to achieve. They go to great lengths to get there and make it happen, but they might be taking some prisoners along the way and think that the end justifies the means. This means that they might overdo it and not lead by example, they might not include other people's viewpoint, or share their train of thought with their team. And they might ignore the signs that it can be done better or that they need to take other things into consideration. All because they're on a mission.

A high achiever might not show good leadership. That can have great personal costs for themselves, and sometimes even the business itself. Their desire to achieve is greater than their desire to perform and align with other functional areas/peers or wider business objectives. They don't obsess as much over why something needs to get done. High achievers are born doers, hard workers, trouble-shooters and problem solvers, but not necessarily diplomats, political or even ethical. They don't have much patience for the status quo if it's not right for them. If you tell them something can't be done, you will likely be ignored. Being so driven means never having a dull moment, but it can be exhausting to never give up or take a proper step back and evaluate along the way. They appear to have something to prove, which usually comes from growing up with adversity or encountering a fair bit of adversity along the way—as we've seen in the first few chapters.

WHAT MAKES HIGH PERFORMERS DIFFERENT?

High performers have all the positive traits of a high achievers and are also driven to make things happen. But they will apply a more holistic view in getting there—including other people's views, considering feedback— and they will be more willing to try to balance that out to get the best outcomes. High performers usually take more time to think, anticipate and prepare the best approach (for example, using the Scenario Thinking Framework™ from Chapter 2), and will let go sooner of an approach that doesn't work. And they will also strive to optimise and fine-tune the best outcomes and tackle issues with more thought and consideration. High performers are usually more effective, or rather, leaders who are in high performance-mode.

You might think this distinction is very subtle, and therefore not important. In my coaching practice, I work with successful leaders who are in leadership roles and who are, most of the time, a high performer. To remain on high performance level is no mean feat. You are not human if you are able to be a high performer all the time. Think about Elon Musk, CEO of Tesla who was reportedly, when he was stressed, sleeping on his factory floor as he thought he didn't have time to go home, shower and recharge. The point he made in the CBS interview with Gayle King, is that he doesn't believe that his people should be experiencing hardship while the CEO is off on vacation. Hence his hands-on approach, to make sure he is doing everything he can. Is that ideal or sustainable?

LEADING IN A "VUCA" WORLD

We all have our flaws, strengths and weaknesses, and our own share of adversity. What's so specific about the volatile, uncertain, complex and ambiguous (VUCA) world we live in is that the adversity or change we can encounter may be new to all of us, so there's no set scenario on how to deal with it. You have to come up with new approaches and know how you can adjust better. To me that's all about self-awareness and knowing what you're made of.

So often my coachees say that they don't have time, or that it's not a priority to think about the bigger picture first. Because of that, they tend to jump into the operational rather than the strategic (which they are required to do in their leadership roles).

For example, a coachee I worked with twice in the last six years has that tendency. When we work on becoming more effective in a VUCA world, it's important to make sure he has the bigger picture first. He is then able to set his priorities correctly, work far more efficiently and focus on achieving them. He can then also delegate better and include and empower his team. You're probably familiar with the idea that when a team feels more autonomy, they will think more for themselves and get more creative and productive.

It's quite frustrating if you are working on an operational matter, to realise when you've put a lot of hours in that you could've handled it smarter and kept up with the strategic demands and kept your team motivated. I can almost guarantee that you're not working at your Peak Performance, but probably struggling through your workload. (In the next chapter, I'll explain what Peak Performance is and how to manage it.)

You not only impact yourself but also your peers, direct reports, your boss and other stakeholders. Agility is key, and to know how to respond with flexibility to change and adversity, you need to build increased adaptability, resilience and creativity. If you are not self-aware, you get into your high achiever mode again instead of your high performer mode. It's easier to adjust when you know what buttons to push. Don't be shy about taking 360-degree assessments, getting feedback and doing self-reflection and introspection. Be willing to do whatever it takes to be more self-aware of how you operate.

HIGH ACHIEVERS HAVE GOOD INTENTIONS, BUT...

We all know them—high achievers and high performers. It's not always fun to work with High achievers because they can be quite obsessive. They will skip lunch or Friday drinks to finish stuff, or they don't share their train of thought which makes it hard to work alongside them or to feel included. When I work with a coachee who is a high achiever, or in high achiever-mode, they usually complain that people don't get it and that they don't get much help, or that they don't think delegating to their team will work. When I then ask the coachee how they have informed the people around them of their idea/plan and progress made and made a detailed request for what they need from the other person and how that could look, they tend to say that takes too much time and that they're better off doing it themselves. But when we work to increase self-awareness and they realise the cost of not delegating or sharing thoughts with the team is too high, there's usually a tipping point. High achievers are then willing to try another approach, as they don't feel like they can progress enough. When they shift their thinking and invest time in dealing with coworkers, they experience the benefits and are keen to do it more often.

A couple of years ago, I worked with a coachee who had been dealing with adversity in her role for some time. When under stress my coachee wasn't used to taking a step back, reflecting and doing some introspection and resetting. She just pushed harder but kept doing the same thing. Due to frustration over not being as effective as usual, her communication style turned more reactive. Instead of being the cheerful people manager she was known as, she became a bit moody and cynical. At that time, she either wasn't aware or had forgotten why she had always been so successful in her role. This recent promotion had come with even more pressure, tight deadlines, conflicting priorities, and a demanding boss. As she was leading the most prestigious project in the business at that time, it was her boss who provided coaching for her.

As her coach, I supported her with first addressing her sense of self-awareness. A 360-degree assessment helped open her eyes to how she perceived herself and how her direct reports, peers, and boss perceived her. It was a true eye-opener for her, as she didn't realise the difference in what she was trying/intended to do and how she came across. She decided that she wanted to improve her behaviour reduce the gap between her own self-perception and the perception people had of her. From there, we focused on her strengths and values, and how she could use them to her advantage to see which of those had been over-underused so far. (More about this in Chapter 6, which deals with strengths.) We also looked at assumptions, beliefs, and habits that didn't serve her anymore.

It's usually not about a lack of good intentions. Most people do the best they can and will have the best intentions. Yet when intentions are not clear or misunderstood, they can have impactful consequences. Often, we find ourselves pursuing certain goals or setting priorities, and your peers might have slightly different ones that can seem like competing instead of aligning priorities. However, to explore intentions and share them by articulating them, the high performer will quickly uncover where the synergy might be found so that you get the best outcomes for all involved. The high achiever, conversely, might push even harder to get to his goals, meet more resistance and maybe ruin good working relationships in the process.

Mind you, most leaders don't consider themselves either a high achiever or a high performer. For them, it's normal to work hard, try to be the best version of themselves and get the best results they can imagine. It's when I start to describe the behaviour that comes with it and the costs that they recognise themselves. Always be aware of your strengths and ask for feedback regularly to realise in which mode you are, high achiever or high performer.

SHIFTING FROM HIGH ACHIEVER TO HIGH PERFORMER WHEN FACING ADVERSITY

Knowing when you are in high achiever or high performer mode makes it easier to know what questions to ask yourself to figure out the next steps. From the definitions in the former chapters, the biggest shift you need to make from high achiever to high performer is to regularly reflect, take a step back and reset (see more in Chapter 7) to keep the bigger picture. By doing this, you'll keep anticipating and including other insights, input and adverse events to make sure the outcome is optimal for all involved.

If you are on autopilot, doing the same thing all over again, nothing good will come of it. There will be consequences. If you keep putting the same in, you'll keep getting the same outcomes. Yes, I'm using this one-liner again, as I see it so often. Taking action is the only change agent. If you don't take action in the form of a new, different approach, you'll end up with an undesirable outcome and you might not have the buy-in you needed—or you might end up having to change things or do it all over again, which is time wasted. And you're not role modelling the most efficient way of working for your team.

A year ago, I spoke to a friend who is also a typical high achiever at times. She resigned from her job as her values were compromised and she had lost all faith and trust in the leadership team she was part of. When she had addressed the way of working with some of her peers one-on-one, they all supported her thoughts but never spoke up during the leadership team meetings. They chose to accept the status quo, keep their heads down and go on autopilot, hoping for better times. Needless to say, my friend didn't accept her status quo for long. Sometimes your gut feeling has given you the sign long ago, but most people want to explore options with their peers. They soon realise that when values are compromised, and it's a culture thing, nothing much will change—especially if the rest of the leadership team is not open for change. The only thing you can do is to be practical and know where you want to go, and what strategy leads to your best outcome that makes you happy. Fast forward to last week. When I spoke to her, she was still happy with her decision and thriving in her new role at a different company.

What she did differently in accepting her current role was to explore the company culture, way of working and values, addressing it explicitly in her job interviews and doing more research to be sure. The more senior your role, the more important that will be. Soft skills—like influencing, getting the buy-in, and convincing people—work better when you share the same/similar values.

Being authentic and true to yourself helps you to articulate how you like to work together, but also you will be more capable of asking and understanding how others intend to work more easily as well. Personally, I find it hard to understand why some company values are so generic, like respect, integrity and trust, as these are big, generic words. You have to ask for specific examples of their values, of what matters to people, and what (way of working) is meaningful to get a better grasp of their culture.

Yes, you can influence culture or the way of working in a big corporate, but it's like trying to change a tanker from its course. If you're a high achiever/performer and you don't have much patience for a status quo that doesn't work for you, make sure you get on a more agile boat that can 'tack' faster. You'll be better off investing time to look elsewhere and taking your time before accepting a new role in a new company, or even a new department within the same company.

When you work on a contract or interim project, you might feel more disassociated, and less attached because you know you have to troubleshoot, consult and then leave after the project is completed. In that case, when a company's way of working or values don't align with yours fully, you can give yourself more flexibility. You might be more willing to accept the status quo, as you know it's temporary.

If you do need to stay in your role for whatever reason and you want to make the most of it, try the 80/20 rule so you can adapt faster and work more effectively, which will elevate fun and fulfilment. The 80/20 rule is also known as the Pareto Principle. According to the principle, roughly 80 percent of the effects come from 20 percent of the causes. For example, in business it could mean that 80 percent of sales come from 20 percent of customers. The way I understand it is that in practice, if you focus your energy on what brings the most relevant benefits, revenue or impact, you are making the most efficient use of your time. With the productivity habits of high achievers—whether they be self-made millionaires, employed highest fee earners or even Olympic athletes—handling every task that gets thrown their way, or even every task that they would like to handle, is impossible. They use the Pareto Principle to help them determine what is of vital importance. Then, they delegate the rest or simply let it go.

For example, if you lead a team in a fast-paced and ever-changing environment, and you're constantly challenged by competing priorities, it's your time and that of your team that you need to maximise. Determine which projects are most important, which align most with the business/company objectives, and what you need to do to align those goals. What part of your business makes up for 80 percent of the revenues and what is the 20 percent of your customer base that generates that revenue? Then focus on that and delegate or drop the rest. Identify what generates 80 percent of your revenue, from which 20 percent of your customer markets. And stick to that. You'll be far more effective than trying to do everything and finding yourself spread too thin in a situation where you also probably achieve less than 80 percent. Stay focused on the bigger picture and spend less time chasing goals that are too farfetched or not immediately relevant. You only have 24 hours in a day. Better to use them wisely and feel fulfilled than waste time and feel frustrated.

It takes courage to have the confidence to make choices and delegate, or even to let things go. As always, the proof is in the pudding. Start simple with a to-do list and try to apply it to a small topic. See where it takes you. Then apply it to bigger topics. You'll build efficiency and better outcomes with practice.

DEFINING AND VISUALISING YOUR DESIRED OUTCOMES (FINETUNING)

In Chapter 2, we spoke about the Scenario Thinking Framework™ and how that works. When it comes to dealing with adversity or setbacks, the first thing you can ask after you have identified that the current situation doesn't work is, "How would I like it to be?" By defining and visualising your best outcomes, you can start strategising, thinking about the best scenario for you. High performers, like elite athletes, visualise what winning would look like. In applying their steps to get there, they will stay very much focused and quite undistracted. High achievers are likely to adopt visualising as well but might not take enough time to anticipate and prepare the most creative and effective steps to get there with inclusion/buy-in from people involved, which high performers often do more of.

If you don't define and describe the desired situation in detail then it's hard to know what your focus should be and how to anticipate, prepare and design the next steps to get there. It is important to visualise your desired outcome because it can help you better understand what it is you want. By writing down keywords that describe the visual, and then reading your described thoughts as words on paper, you can feel more connected to the material and create a more personal experience. A couple of well-known benefits are:

- It improves your performance
- It helps you reach your potential
- It reduces stress
- It brings more fulfilment into your life
- It increases focus
- It can spark inspiration and new ideas
- It boosts confidence

I really like that it helps you reach your potential. For me the reason to write this book is to help people with being the best version of themselves they can be. I sure am striving to be the best version I can be, especially when adversity is thrown at me. And I've experienced firsthand what it is to visualise and to write down my thoughts for more impact and to make those ideas come alive. Specifically, when I was recovering from injuries, I was visualising how it would look if I could be mobile again, meeting clients face to face again, instead of via the phone. It does increase my fulfilment of trying to figure out next steps, like doing exercises in my case. And then when you do take those first next steps and it brings you closer to your desired outcome, how good does that feel? That you know you have turned things around for yourself when you go again on your first face-to-face client meeting. Or when you have turned things around for others, in the best possible way, with the least effort and biggest benefits. It truly does spike my confidence, reduces my stress levels, increases my energy and urges me to try more of it. And I've seen so many other people I work with do it, from which I learn even more. Try it out and let me know what the impact is for you? My point is that when you face adversity, and you fine-tune and visualise next steps and how it can look, you can turn things around and turn it into an advantage.

As a leader, if you can't articulate where you are going, chances are that people will find it hard to follow you and contribute to your ideal outcome. It's about inclusion and making others part of your train of thought, but also having that clear and compelling vision filled with purpose—knowing what it would allow you and how it would contribute to your ideal outcome. Through this, you will know what it would allow you and the team/business if you achieved your goal. Without visualisation, it remains vague and unattainable. It's also a great feeling to cross things off your list: done, next task.

I work with many leaders who know, in broad terms, where they're heading because it's in the company/business plan, or there are certain targets or revenues set, or it's set out in their mission statement. But that's high level and not what I mean. It only becomes more meaningful when you focus more on the specifics and visuals.

And, of course, this is where beliefs, positive thinking and framing come into play.

For instance, one of my coachees wanted to have a sign-off for his strategic plan and budget. He told me he had discussed and emailed his boss several times but either didn't get a response or not the response he wanted, and he needed to progress. We started to unpack how his approach had been so far:

- He needed the sign off as he then had to invest money in new resources and investing in services from certain vendors.
- There were still decisions to make and choices for either one approach or the other.
- In his communication to his boss he had mentioned all the variables and asked for what his boss thought about them. (However, his boss might think: "This is what I hired YOU for.")

When I asked him what the ideal outcome to his comms/emails was supposed to be, he said, "I only want to have the sign-off, like—'OK, yes, go ahead!'" Although you might be able to visualise this, it makes more sense to be specific. So, I challenged him to adapt his communications and be more specific in what he would suggest, what response he needed from his boss, and when.

It became clear to him that he needed to rewrite his email in such a way that the only response from his boss could be, "Yes, go ahead!" When we discussed this, he also visualised the email he would receive and the smile on his own face when looking in the mirror. That's when he felt relief. It was much clearer how he should change his email and his suggestions, making it much clearer what he would suggest as the way forward, close the email with his preferable approach and get a sign-off on that. When he sent his revised email, it took his boss two minutes to reply with, "Yes, go for it!" That brought a huge smile to his face.

Another benefit of visualisation was discussed by Dr. Maxwell Maltz, in the internationally bestselling classic Psycho-Cybernetics that has inspired and enhanced the lives of more than 30 million readers. He noted: "Your subconscious cannot tell the difference between a real memory, and a vividly imagined visualisation." As such when you visualise you effectively "implant" new memories into your self-image—meaning that your subconscious mind "thinks" you are already the success you dream of being. This frees up subconscious resources to help you reach your goals, and it also increases confidence, sometimes dramatically."

If you'd like to read more about it, Tony Robbins (in his book *Unlimited Power*) describes Maltz' book in a great way, using my favourite metaphor, sailing:

"When loosely translated from the Greek, cybernetics means 'a helmsman who steers his ship to port.' Psycho-Cybernetics, a term coined by Dr. Maxwell Maltz, means, 'steering your mind to a productive, useful goal so you can reach the greatest port in the world, peace of mind'. Maltz was the first researcher and author to explain how the self-image (a term he popularised) has complete control over an individual's ability to achieve (or fail to achieve) any goal. And he developed techniques that anyone can use to improve and manage self-image - visualisation, mental rehearsal, relaxation. These techniques have informed and inspired countless motivational gurus, sports psychologists, and self-help practitioners for more than fifty years. The teachings of Psycho-Cybernetics are timeless because they are based on solid science and provide a prescription for thinking and acting that leads to quantifiable results. According to Maxwell Maltz, "Psycho-Cybernetics occurs when the mind has a defined target, so that it can focus and direct and refocus and redirect until it reaches its intended goal." In terms of adversity there might not be one specific approach to deal with it, but if you keep fine-tuning your approach, you will calm your mind, and get more creative in getting to your best outcome. (See more in Chapter 8, on neuroscience.)

Furthermore, by describing and visualising, it's all about positive use of words and positive mindset. For example, you would write down, "I want this, I need this or that," and not. "I don't want, or I don't need A or B." From a positive wording and mindset, it's far easier to come up with the next steps. You feel excited about how it could look, you get more creative and it's usually more in your control than something you don't want— which is under the control of someone or something else.

Try to describe for yourself in detail what the best outcome would be. Don't go overboard when I say in detail—keep it real but make it compelling and meaningful for you, so that you literally start to get the picture. Describe the desired outcome in positive words as well as in visuals. You will be motivated by the joy or excitement you get from 'seeing' your outcome come to life on paper or in your mind. Every step you take will be focused on that, so you will be able to be as efficient as possible.

Don't take too much time and go in too much detail to define and visualise your ideal or desired outcome. Think 80/20 and move on when you feel that it's starting to come alive.

ONLY ACCEPT THE STATUS QUO THAT'S RIGHT FOR YOU - AS A HIGH ACHIEVER OR A HIGH PERFORMER

People with similar DNA makeup (a high achiever and a high performer) will decide differently on when the status quo is not right for them, and what they are willing to do about it. Whether their actions will serve themselves and others involved plays a key role.

It's interesting to look at this from a leader's point of view, dealing with his direct reports. It's important to know if you're dealing with a high achiever or a high performer so that you know what works when you respond. To tell a high achiever that something can't be done is like talking to the wall. The high achiever will then get resourceful and prove you wrong, but you could have benefited if you'd realised that high achievers are hard on themselves and don't usually allow themselves a break—for fear of losing momentum and progress. In your approach to this person, use your empathy, and offer to take a step back and brainstorm together for a more effective approach and direction. Then they will become interested. High achievers find it hard to ask for help, but when it's offered in a direct way, it's usually welcomed.

If the direct report is a high performer then guidance is more effective—they will listen to your reasoning and arguments and will come back with their approach after they have thought it through and weighed up several options. They usually will take a step back and take the time to plan, as they know they will win back efficiency in the long run.

High achievers will usually not linger when a status quo doesn't serve them. But they are prone to draw conclusions faster, make assumptions or cut corners. For a high achiever, accepting a status quo that's *not* right for them makes no sense. They know they have the resources to come up with a way around the adversity or setback.

A high performer, however, will weigh the arguments and interests of others and will have a better outlook on future events. They know that if they act too soon and too impulsively, they may find themselves at a new impasse. A high performer is also a little bit more strategic in approach and is equally happy when they don't have many obstacles in their way—as they will then further focus on the empowerment of their team and find synergy with peers, more than high achievers would do.

A coachee I worked with was lacking confidence in their ability to be eligible for promotion. They had become impatient with the lack of growth opportunities. She was the director of a department in a big company and she was aiming to become the director of a broader business unit. In her impatience to get there, she decided to be proactive and made a presentation about what she would do if she were given the position. Organising a meeting with her two bosses was taking a long time, and as time went by her confidence decreased and anxiety set in. Hadn't she done all the work? Hadn't she shown by the results that she was up for it? Didn't they tell her when they hired her that this was a realistic pathway? She wasn't happy with the status quo anymore and was trying to force their hands to change it. When she finally got the meeting, they weren't interested in her presentation. However, she got the job—accompanied by a transition coaching program and certain milestones as objectives. She was told that they believed she could do the job, but that she needed to work on her approach for buy-in.

If she would have shifted more to a high performer approach, she would have saved herself the time of preparing a presentation and, using the Scenario Thinking Framework™ and visualisation, she could have been better prepared and better anticipated what the delay was. With that information, she could have shown the bigger picture and anticipated how she would start the new role, and with what focus, and get her buy-in. She would have started the new role with a feeling of validation and renewed energy and confidence. Instead, she felt she had to prove herself first and get through "probation." The good side of her high achiever's DNA was that she didn't waste any time, took feedback to heart and showed them she could grow in her role in a more effective way. The "bad" side was that it didn't quite get her there so smoothly.

Fear of getting a no and overplaying your hand might keep people from that promotion but on the other hand, if you don't ask, you don't get. In this example, there were many other developments going on in the broader company, which is why the conversation didn't have priority for her bosses, but they had decided months ago she would be the best for the role. If she had addressed the issue earlier, they might have told her and she would have had peace of mind, however none of them were proactive on the topic.

There are always exceptions to the rule, but my point is that if you always start big picture and first put yourself in other's shoes first, it will help you understand how any action will impact your position and what the best approach will be.

I always urge my coachees: if the status quo isn't right for you, *address* the issues with your boss, peers, leadership team or board. Make sure you seek to understand before you take off in a direction that might not be beneficial or takes longer to get to where you want to be. As high achievers are not risk averse, they usually are willing to address issues or have a "confrontation"—as long as they anticipate and prepare for the conversation and aren't reactive or act impulsively.

Find your courage, reflect and take time to do your Scenario Thinking™, and align to the bigger picture. Include not only your personal strategy but also that of the business.

CHAPTER CONCLUSION

No situation is the same, and we all have different DNA makeup. That's why the Scenario Thinking Framework™ is such a powerful tool to help you get clarity and take the next step.

High achievers and high performers are different. Sometimes these differences in approach are subtle, but often there's a huge difference in effectiveness and efficiency. When using The Scenario Thinking

Framework™ you remain critical of yourself. You investigate the course you have set out to achieve, whether your goals and objectives are still the right ones, and how they align with the bigger picture of the business/company. As there's change around you constantly, you need to keep your eyes open and keep reflecting regularly. The Scenario Thinking Framework™, the Pareto Principle (the 80/20 rule) and visualisation will help you. Whether you tend to be in high achiever or high performer mode, you will be more well-rounded and effective when taking the above into consideration, and will build better relationships and buy-in along the way.

Know what you're made of, become more self-aware and keep reflecting so that you can always find the most effective approach in every situation. Leaders in fast-changing environments need to constantly adapt and, for that, they need to keep evolving. If you're not aware of how you're tracking in that process, you might not have the most effective approach. If the status quo is not right for you, stop and think before you respond or act. The Scenario Thinking Framework™ must be in your muscle and on top of mind as your go-to-tool.

It might seem like hard work, but it's so worth it. Is there a next level to increasing your adaptability and working more effortlessly? Yes, there is. Keep reading. In the next chapter, you will learn how to manage and maintain your peak performance or flow and spend more time in high performance mode. It's the ultimate shift from high achiever to high performer as we become more experienced and resourceful, and we flag what our options are sooner, when we encounter adversity and/or a status quo that doesn't work for us. Who doesn't want that?

MANAGING AND MAINTAINING YOUR PEAK PERFORMANCE

(Featuring my interview with Carolijn Brouwer, Volvo Ocean Race veteran and Rolex World Sailor of the Year 2018)

If you keep doing the same thing, you keep getting the same outcomes (remember?) You must have a growth mindset and a continued hunger for learning, to keep evolving and making progress.

Striving for peak performance (which is generally also called being in flow, or in flow state, having a runner's high, being in the zone etc.) is not a luxury or for elite athletes only, nor is it something unattainable. It's for everyone who wants to be the best they can be. And it's different for everyone. But you have to put in the work, and it doesn't just require perseverance and determination, which most high achievers have in spades. It also requires a deep self-awareness of how you can get to being your best self.

When should it matter to you to know whether you are performing at peak, or in flow state? When you're serious about improving and optimising your leadership skills and the high performance of yourself and your team, evolving and making progress. Next to knowing your personal DNA make up and self-awareness, knowing how to shift from high achiever to high performer mode and how to manage your peak performance will be one of the most important tools in your toolbox.

Jamie Wheal, co-founder and Executive Director of the Flow Genome Project, expert on peak performance and leadership, specialises in the neuroscience and application of flow states. He explains flow brilliantly in a YouTube video published on Dec 26, 2013, "Hacking the GENOME of Flow: Jamie Wheal at TEDxVeniceBeach."

For the purpose of this book, I will introduce my translation/summary of his findings. He mentions that when we're in flow, we are selfless, we perform effortlessly, and our sense of time slows down or speeds up. Selfless meaning: we loose our sense of self, we don't listen to our inner critic, we don't suffer from self-doubt, we are not/less inhibited. Effortless meaning: we accelerate our learning and mastery much faster than normally. And because we are so much enjoying what we are doing, we forget about time passing: time either seems to slow down or speed up, because we are so focused on the task at hand, and passes by without us noticing. This state, when action and awareness merge and where we are both do-ers and be-ers, as Jamie explains, is when we are in flow or peak performance.

Flow is one of the four states we go through regarding performance and using our brains, more specifically: activating certain brainwaves. It's a highly addicting state, but also contagious, in the sense that we can motivate or role model effective behaviours for others by demonstrating that being in flow is performing at our best and having fun.

The four states are:

1. Struggle state
2. Release state
3. Flow state
4. Recovery state

Back to Struggle again etc

Let me begin with Struggle state. Although Struggle state sounds a bit tough, it's actually your launch path into Flow state. In Struggle state you work out how to tackle or deal with a problem, or anticipate a conversation or meeting. It is in this state that using the Scenario Thinking Framework™ is most helpful. This is where we struggle to perform at our best. We are suffering and pushing to get through, and to achieve the results we want, trying to solve a problem. This is where our inner critics are at work; our self-doubt, stress and frustration pops up. And sometimes we feel we are not creative or productive anymore, but just going around in circles with our thoughts. And when we have enough of that and we get exhausted, we must take a step back and stop with what we're doing.

That is when we relax which prompts a release in our brains and we shift from Beta to Alpha brainwaves. This is the Release state. You literally take your mind of things, go for a walk or grab some coffee. When we pick things up again, we have renewed insights and energy to apply and find ourselves in flow, for example due to a surge of creativity because we relaxed and looked at things differently. That's when the dopamine tends to kick in which makes us feel that we need to do more of it: "we're on to something.." And the release of endorphins even makes us feel no or less pain, so that we keep on going.

When we are in flow experiencing Theta/Gamma brainwaves, we feel and perform optimally and lateral thinking (commonly known as "out of the box" thinking, recognising and merging different patterns together) is possible. However, this flow state doesn't last long.

When we go to sleep, we're in Recovery state and this is where the real learning happens, during the deep Delta brain waves. Of course, it's hard to sleep during your working hours, but try mindfulness instead, to calm the mind and reset yourself (also see Chapter 7). What I find interesting as well is that Jamie mentions the phrase "Transient Hypofrontality" that takes place in our brain when we are in flow, which silences our inner critic. And again this indicates that it's a state that comes and goes, as Transient in this context means: "for a little while," Hypo means: "not a lot of" and Frontality refers to the complex PFC (prefrontal cortex, also known as the executive function of the brain, where decisions are made etc.). Jamie explains that our PFC goes offline when we are in flow, which clarifies why we can perform without inhibitions.

This cycle shows that it's really important to acknowledge that we have to go through all four states to keep up getting into peak performance again and again: you must have renewed energy to "struggle" at the task/ challenge at hand again, finding and improving solutions. You need to take a break and step back regularly to recharge, get into Release state, to get into flow again where you perform optimally, effortlessly. Then you need to recover from that effort of being in flow, consolidating the learnings during Recovery state, and then to be able to start with new "struggles' for new problems etc.

Recharge (Release state) and sleep or mindfulness (Recovery state) are so important in this cycle. Giving up on your new ideas or approach, only to fall back on your old approaches, doesn't give you a fresh, and more effective or innovative take on things. But to persevere in your efforts, you need to step away now and then, recharge and sleep well to recover enough, to start the next day with a new "struggle," coming up with new ideas and fresh perspectives. I come across a lot of coachees who are trying to keep up, shifting from Struggle to Flow state and back again. Think back to my example of Elon Musk in Chapter 1. The reason I mentioned him is that he's such a high performer and capable of coming up with fantastic innovative solutions. Yet even when he doesn't take a step back regularly and doesn't sleep, it will be difficult to keep pushing on and perform in flow. It will come at a high personal cost regarding your wellbeing. It's not sustainable.

Jamie's colleague, Steven Kotler, co-founder and Director of Research for the Flow Genome Project, describes in his highly entertaining New York Times bestselling book *The Rise of Superman*: "The one element that truly sets flow apart is the creative, problem solving nature of this state. Because flow requires action—otherwise action and awareness cannot merge—there's decision making involved in every step." And he concludes that "flow is an extremely efficient and effective decision-making strategy." Which Jamie underlines with: "Flow is the largest driver of innovation, scientific breakthroughs, and top athlete performance peaks." And I fully agree.

Can you imagine my excitement reading all this? How empowering this is for everyone and specifically for leaders in fast-paced and ever-changing organisations that we can manage our peak performance. We can optimise our decision making, increasing our adaptability to adversity and building further resilience.

My take on Jamie's and Steven's above findings is that, when you're in flow, you:

- Are in an optimal state of consciousness with minimal distractions
- Are your best and happy self
- Are in an intense, focused and concentrated state in the present moment

- Have a minimum of (negative) self-talk, self-consciousness or self-doubt
- Have clear goals and steps, learn faster and are more creative and productive
- Are experiencing flow, fun, and fulfilment

To give you a simple example, when I was writing this book, I was in flow when I had silenced my phone, iPad and other distractions. When I'd done my research for a chapter and had a clear goal what the chapter should involve, I lost track of time and progressed well. I regularly took a step back to recharge. I felt very enthusiastic, excited and fulfilled when the chapter was done. When I reflected on this, it was my preparation, together with the belief that I can help others perform better through this book, which drove me. I also enjoyed the process. Because "without fun, peak performance is practically impossible," according to Friederike Fabritius, MS and Hans M. Hagemann, PHD in their book *The Leading Brain, neuroscience hacks to work smarter, better, happier.* Friederieke and Hans explain in their book that "when you have fun, your brain releases Dopamine, which is associated with pleasure, addiction and reward and triggered by excitement, novelty and risk. Dopamine is involved in your ability to update information in memory and also affects your ability to focus on the task at hand. That's why Dopamine is also known as a novelty neurotransmitter. Last but not least Dopamine is the D in DNA of Peak Performance: Dopamine, Noradrenaline and Acetylcholine." In short, "Noradrenaline's primary purpose is to ensure your survival. It regulates your attention and alertness, and it's at an optimal level when you feel slightly over challenged or pushing yourself to perform a difficult task better, faster or with fewer resources. Acetylcholine helps our learning for new information and babies are the best example for that: they are the most alert and observant little people on the planet, who soak up new stimuli like sights, sounds, smell and taste for continuous and cognitive learning."

My research on peak performance led me to read about scientists, elite athletes. and well-known artists and musicians and how they do their best work. What they had in common was that they all built up their skills in a slow, deliberate and methodical way, with minimal interruptions, regular practice and finetuning, recovery and discipline. And, of course, they had found something they were passionate about and wanted to become better at. Through their increased skill, they aim to help others, entertain, thrill or move others in a way that benefits both them and their audience.

HOW TO AVOID SHIFTING BACK TO HIGH ACHIEVER

When you are in high performance or peak performance or flow state, you need to realise that it is literally a state. As I described before, there are four states which you tend to go cycle through: Struggle, Release, Flow and Recovery. A state comes and goes. It doesn't last but you can alert, train and remind yourself to go back to that state more often. When you feel yourself shifting back to Struggle state without much release or recovery built into the cycle, which particularly high achievers tend to do, at first, that is not something to be too alarmed about. It's just not the most effective state of performance, if you would remain there.

As a person and as a leader, wouldn't you want to be your best self as much as possible? Some "gentle" adversity, which helps us to reset and sharpen ourselves and also to appreciate success or happiness is not such a bad thing. But, of course, I would like to feel at the top of my game most of the time, if I can help it, without adversity. And yes, if I can, you can too.

The impact of knowing how to avoid shifting back is massive. It will do wonders for your confidence levels. Your creativity and productivity will go up whilst you get to your desired state and goals faster. But let's not forget about having that deep self-belief, which is another benefit of the flow state, and is a great driver for top athletes. You need to know what you're made of and how to use your strengths, knowledge, experience, and purpose. Keep finetuning and focussing, learning and reading about what you like to do better, know more of, and yes, also enjoy the journey.

Shifting back to high achiever or Struggle state often happens unconsciously. In these states, particularly spending too much time in Struggle state, you're not being your best or most effective self when it comes to contributing to the bigger whole. It might be because you encounter a setback, hurdle or some adversity that demotivates you, puts pressure on you and wears you down. This puts a dent in your confidence and your progress will be interrupted. You need to address and flag what's happening in order to deal with it. Sometimes people keep going, as they like to ignore it and hope the adversity goes away. It takes energy to deal with it, and sometimes we just don't feel like shifting gears again. And hey, we're only human.

When we are struggling at work finding a solution for a problem or deciding on a certain issue, the adrenaline that first kicked in to make us pay attention has outlasted its purpose and we're heading into exhaustion and frustration. Time to do something about it. Time to take a step back, recharge and refresh, and then try to get back into flow and avoid shifting back to your high achiever's mode. Of course, being in high achiever's mode is not equal to Struggle state, but it's not the most effective leadership approach for everyone (other than chasing your goals).

When we try to avoid shifting back to high achiever mode, we're aiming for high performer mode or flow state. However, as we know there is an in-between station called the Release state. You get there because you are actively taking a step back—taking a walk or "sleeping on it" and letting your struggling thoughts go for a while. Yes, that's right, you cut yourself some slack. That's not easy for leaders who are usually hard on themselves. But you need to change gears in order to get to flow state. The benefit of the Release state is that your agitated Beta brainwaves start slowing down to Alpha brainwaves, which takes stress hormones out of your system. You can literally breathe easier and become less worried about the problem. Because of that you get more creative and productive, and you're on the doorstep of the flow state: you're engaged in something but not pushing yourself too hard. When you have that sensation, you're on to something and realise that you need to keep doing it because it feels great. This will boost your lateral thinking, giving you those 'Aha!' moments and insights. And there you go: you pushed the turbo button, as Wheal calls it, and you are on top of your game and going into flow state again.

Whenever you stress out because you think about a fearful future ("I'm not able to pull it off") or a fearful past ("It happened to me before"), make sure to read Chapter 7 on the psychological and physical exercises you can do to alleviate those feelings. We all know that meditation, mindfulness, breathing exercises or exercising have a calming effect on our minds. When you have that sense of calm in the Release state, you can become more creative again and go back into flow state.

Lack of sleep, feeling stressed, hangry and lethargic? Eat your food in a mindful way, and eat regularly (refuel), take your rest (your body needs eight to nine hours of sleep), drink water to hydrate throughout the day and be more present. It sounds so obvious, but are you taking enough care of yourself in that way? Going back to basics, letting go and recharging is always a good idea and prevents you from shifting back. Treat yourself well and move with less pain and suffering and more effortless with more efficiency.

Self-awareness is key here. As you no doubt know, DNA is your genetic make-up and I use it here as a metaphor for the unique aspects of your personality. Knowing your personal "DNA" makeup is crucial. Ask for feedback regularly and explore what your strengths and values are on a regular basis, and how you're using them (see Chapter 6). Know how you show up, meaning how people perceive you when they interact with you. Know what you want to achieve and seek out other people's opinions to take into consideration. In Dr Tasha Eurich's article on *HBR. org*, "What Self-Awareness Really is (and How to Cultivate it)" published on January 04, 2018, she quotes research that suggests that "when we see ourselves clearly, we are more confident and more creative. We make sounder decisions, build stronger relationships, and communicate more effectively. We're less likely to lie, cheat, and steal. We are better workers who get more promotions. And we're more effective leaders with more satisfied employees and more profitable companies."

Adversity, hurdles and setbacks come in all shapes. The better you know yourself, the better you can shift between states. And, in general, do more of what makes you feel alive.

WE CAN'T ALWAYS BE IN FLOW

Adversity gets in the way and flow comes and goes. But how you deal with it is what will speed up your recovery time. You know, after reading the start of this chapter, how to shift back from your high achievers- mode when you encounter adversity. Now, how can you deal with it in a way that reduces your recovery time, or your ineffectiveness in your leadership?

In the first part of this chapter, I described the four states in the cycle of peak performance or flow. We go in and out of those states, including the flow state. When you're out of the flow state, you would ideally go into the necessary Recovery state. This is where all your experience and knowledge will be stored and structured in your brain's memory. But at the same time, when you get out of your natural high, typical high achievers and high performers might start to feel down as they are not as effective as before and they are pretty hard on themselves. This is when people tell you to celebrate the wins.

Reflect on how far you've come, bask in your glory a bit and consider that if you have already achieved that, imagine what more you can achieve? Reflection and introspection are quite healthy whilst your brain recovers. But what often happens is that the next adversity or big challenge announces itself and we jump straight in. This is a fast-track to Struggle state, not permitting ourselves to do some anticipation or solid preparation, or using your Scenario Thinking Framework™. The better you deal with managing the state you're in, the faster your recharging recovery time.

A coachee I worked with—a seasoned leader and people manager—

explained his situation as follows: "I switched from enjoying to hating my role, up to the point that I feel totally overwhelmed. It's just too much to juggle: work, travel, board work, family, kids, friends, sports, etc." I asked him how he recharges, and he said he didn't have time for that. I helped him to see that when he doesn't take enough recovery time, and when he dips in and out of Flow and back to Struggle state, he isn't managing himself effectively—he is purely reacting and surviving; dealing with adversity, pressure, and obligations. He was keen to experience the different states and their benefits more consciously, become more effective and build in more recovery time, to bounce back faster from struggling with adversity or a high workload.

What made a difference was that he was open to a different approach, having a growth mindset. Going forward, he used positive framing when thinking about what he was after but also in conversations with others. He started to anticipate and prepare better using the Scenario Thinking Framework™, and he used one of his strengths—humour—more. This had a huge impact on the people around him, and they started to enjoy working with him. He found that delegating and getting his buy-in became easier as well. By changing his state of mind to "it's only work," he found space in his head to let go of worries and was able to deal with it head on and ask for help sooner. Increasing his awareness of what drove him and where his strengths were made it easier to manage his states, and he learnt to move from one to the other with more control.

Sorry but no, there's no set formula. I wish there was, but we are all different people and what works for one person doesn't always work for another. However, reflecting on what you're made of and how you usually achieve a successful and effective outcome helps. Take the time for reflection as it usually pays off.

We are all creatures of habits, beliefs and assumptions. It's tough to break away from them when they don't serve you anymore, especially in a new situation or in a situation of adversity. You need to realise that it all starts within yourself. Change your state and you'll get different responses and outcomes. But what to change and where to start? Sometimes it's easier to have someone else hold a mirror and challenge your thoughts. Reach out to a friend, coach or mentor for some tough love and guidance. And start acting on the above hacks.

Don't make excuses that you don't have time. If you don't change your approach, nothing will happen, or it will become worse. Investing time in yourself, enhancing the ways you operate, taking rest, thinking and talking to yourself will pay off and will win you time as you get more effective. You will speed up your recovery time and move more easily to flow state again.

PARALLELS BETWEEN ADVERSITY AND LEADERSHIP IN TOP-LEVEL SAILING AND BUSINESS

Leadership, teamwork, and effectiveness in business have many parallels in sport. The more senior you become in an organisation, the more it comes down to you to make decisions, solve problems, motivate people and set the course. However, rather than being operational, you're now more strategic. Soft skills like influencing, negotiating and positioning are essential to get you to where you want to be. And wouldn't you like to thrive doing that, rather than to survive?

If you are a high achiever or a high performer, chances are you like your sports. Of course, there are other things you might be interested in like arts, music, ballet, etc., but often, you really enjoy that top level of achievement. If you feel you need to up your game, sometimes reading about others excelling in sports or arts as a metaphor explains leadership best. How does your sailing or tennis idol keep going when facing adversity and how do they adapt and bounce back? Being inspired by people who seem to achieve the unthinkable and make it look so easy is a great source of inspiration. See if you can use their ways, translating them for your new approach in your leadership role.

Adversities in life can be turned into an advantage (see Chapter 1) to make you excel in high-pressure situations, whether it's in sports or business. When people consider them as growth opportunities and reap the learnings from it for future benefit, it will help them to thrive. That doesn't mean you now need to look for adversity, but it does mean that we shouldn't be afraid to encounter adversity or to fail in our attempts to be and do better.

As with any mastery, to excel as a leader requires a keenness for continuous learning and self-improvement. We all know success doesn't happen overnight. But if you have faced adversities, you might as well use them to your benefit.

I can't say it enough: Reflection and awareness are very important.

Ask yourself how you dealt with adversity before—whether in life, sports or business. How did you deal with it and what can you learn from that approach, so that you know whether to do more or less of a certain approach the next time you face adversity? If this reflection becomes a habit, you will start to improve your approaches, and increase your adaptability, resilience and decision making. Next time you or someone in your team finds themselves in adversity, you will become more confident and creative in order to deal with it, and hence more effective. Don't let a situation like that linger. Remind yourself that the faster you deal with adversity, the faster you will progress.

Chris Smith, the founder and CEO of Athlete Network gave an interview to the American magazine *Entrepreneur* in 2015, where he talked about the "5 Things About Overcoming Adversity That Athletes Can Teach Entrepreneurs." To summarise, the five things are:

- Flexibility is key
- Persistence pushes you to the next level
- Mental fortitude helps push past obstacles
- Put it all in perspective
- Have humility

Flexibility in business has to do with adaptability. How flexible are you to adapt to changing conditions, adversity, setbacks, unexpected situations? And do you then use your awareness of your DNA make up to decide how to best use your persistence, without just keep pushing and struggling? What has resilience taught you to bounce back after adversity or in the face of obstacles? Have the bigger picture. How does your goal sit in the bigger scheme of things? Keep fine-tuning and adjusting the required perspective. And being humble is not about not being able to celebrate wins and be proud of an achievement, but it's about being aware that you never stop learning. The more you know, the more you'll be aware you don't know that much and that there's still so much to learn in your field. That is, if you want to be the best you can be and contribute in the best possible way. Translating sporting metaphors for your application to business doesn't need to be too complicated. The same skills are required, and more so: action is always required.

INTERVIEW:
DUTCH WORLD CHAMPIONSHIP SAILOR, CAROLIJN BROUWER

What we can learn from top athletes on how to deal with adversity and to stay/get back into peak performance is further illustrated in the following interview I had with Dutch world champion sailor, Carolijn Brouwer.

Dutch sailor Carolijn Brouwer, age 45 years, was the 2018 Rolex World Sailor of the Year, Twice ISAF (International Sailing Federation) World Sailor of the Year Award Winner Volvo Ocean Race, four times World Champion, Sports Woman of the Year 2018 WISP (World of Women in Sports, for elite athletes) three times Olympic Games, three times Volvo Ocean Race, Winner of the 2017-2018 Volvo Ocean Race with Dongfeng Race Team, was the first woman to win the race, and Helmsman for the Wild Oats X or Ocean Respect Sailing, an all-female team in The Sydney-Hobart Race of 2018, finishing second on handicap and sixth on line honours, all whilst spreading the message of sustainability and care for our oceans.

Carolijn's Dongfeng yacht in action during the Volvo Ocean Race 2017/18
PHOTOGRAPH BY ELOI STICHELBAUT

Carolijn is quite familiar with adversity as an elite athlete, competing in the most challenging sailing races on earth. She is at her best in the role of helmsman and trimmer. Her story shows us how important it is to have a growth mindset, to know your strengths and to keep adjusting your behaviours and beliefs to achieve peak performance as part of a team.

Carolijn tells about her experience in the Volvo Ocean Race 2017/18 (VOR), a long, gruelling yacht race around the world, which is held every three years. She describes it as "a big rollercoaster of highs and lows. It is the longest race in the history of sport. There is no other race in the world that takes nine months."

Carolijn explains: "Like any race, preparation is key to success. But how do you prepare both physically and mentally for a race that will last nine months? It's the time you spend together as a team that makes the difference. We had about eight months of preparation before the start of the race. You spend more time with each other than with your own family. You work out in the gym together, you eat together, you train together, you do briefings together, and you have dinner together. And you repeat it all again the next day for six days a week.

You get to know each other's strengths and weaknesses and you complement each other, creating a strong bond that prepares you for adversity.

The good times are easy, it's dealing with the bad times—and every team encounters them in their own way—is what make it hard. Also having all the heads pointing in the same direction helps a lot. You have to have a goal, and everyone involved needs to be chasing that same goal. Having a clear shared goal is extremely important."

THE ADVERSITY FOR CAROLIJN AND HER TEAM

"During the 2017/2018 edition of the VOR, a life was lost at sea. John Fisher, crew member of Team Sun Hung Kai/Scallywag, fell overboard in the treacherous high seas of the Southern Ocean and his body was never recovered. The man overboard situation did not occur on our boat but when the life of a fellow sailor is lost at sea, it affects everybody. We were all in shock and didn't know whether to continue racing or stop racing. But when you are in the Southern Ocean you cannot stop, you are in the middle of nowhere, and you have to keep going, for the safety of your boat and your team.

We arrived in Itajai, Brazil in 2nd place and moved up to 1st overall. We were especially relieved that we had balanced that tough leg well between how hard we could push the boat in the rough conditions and when we had to throttle back and sail slower (which for a team is harder than sailing fast), for the safety of boat and crew."

How did you deal with it and what were the learnings or insights?

"What got me through this physically and mentally tough leg in the race, besides trust and respect towards each other, is to be confident that you can believe that the person next to you is the best person for the job and you need to trust them that they will do the job just as well as you, or preferably even better. You have to visualise yourself at the end of the race and be able to look at your crew mates next to you and be proud that you are standing next to them on the highest podium. If a person has made a mistake, don't point fingers, instead help by sharing experiences with each other to keep learning and growing as a team and that builds the confidence.

With the loss of John Fisher we also received support from our shore team who had prepared a personal video with messages from our close family and friends reminding us why we were there and why we were doing this. It made us all very emotional, but it helped in the mourning process and getting back into racing mode. We learned that we needed to be even more patient, keep communicating with each other. We had to keep anticipating and change gears taking new decisions with the team. We had to keep believing in our performance and trust our decisions and support each other in those decisions. We had entered the second half of the nine-month race and other teams would start showing signs of fatigue and lack of motivation and this is where we had to trust our preparation and stay focused and strong. We had to keep reminding ourselves what we came to do and what our goal was and that was to win the VOR. I had already sailed around the world before in a former VOR, and so we were all specifically selected by the Skipper for our will to win, and on how we dealt with adversity individually and as a team.

What fuelled my perseverance was that you're not doing it for yourself but for the team (the whole team—so also the team we leave on shore). And what also helped was the idea that the rest of the fleet was in the same situation ("in the same boat"), but that we were stronger.

The communication and feedback loop between the Skipper, Helmsman and Trimmer (Carolijn) were very important in this situation. As a team, you can't just focus on your own individual performance like during the

Carolijn Brouwer with the "Volvo Ocean Race 2017/18" trophy.
PHOTOGRAPH BY ELOI STICHELBAUT

Olympics where the focus was on me and my boat, but you need to be aware and make sure that everyone can do their piece of the puzzle at their best. Which was very important and a constant focus for me. We kept finetuning, both our decision making and performance.

Another factor that makes a high-performance team is the strong quality that a Skipper as the leader needs to demonstrate—which he did—being humble. In these ever changing, dangerous conditions, where it can be about life or death, the Skipper needs to rely on his team and be able to ask for help if he doesn't know the best approach. Asking for help and relying on the team that they can step up and that we can work it out together is an empowering shift. Being authentic as a leader is also important to me. It makes it easier to know when to reset, or to help someone to reset. Making sure eating and sleeping was more balanced, for better decision making and morale."

What behaviours did you role model to help others?
"Showing positive energy, trusting and respecting each other, never giving up, staying within your strengths and being humble were the most important behaviours that helped us as a team to do well. You have to know your strengths and how you contribute to the team. I stepped up if I felt I could mediate between two people arguing. As a people person I really care about people's wellbeing, so motivating others/encouraging them, suggesting different approaches comes naturally to me and I guess my composure helps others in stressful situations."

What mindset helped you in dealing with the adversity?
"Remaining level-headed and laser focused. Keeping motivation and determination up, coupled with trust, respect and solid leadership were the main elements. In challenging circumstances, you have to take decisions in a split second. Being confident that you can use your intuition in that moment is crucial. Using your adrenaline to enhance your thinking and the situation. Adjust the focus from someone making a mistake, from

blaming them, to reminding the team of the bigger picture: the shared goal, winning. Being open to feedback and learning from the previous leg: With the help of our on-shore team we analysed the data of the boat on how we were tracking and what we could do better."

What will these learnings allow you(r team) next time when facing adversity?

"It will allow us to trust and rely on each other more and stay focused on our goal. When we decided as a team to continue racing, we put safety first. I reflected, reset and we communicated well about the situation. We were even more aligned and determined as a team."

It doesn't matter if you face adversity in elite sports, business or in your personal life, the better we deal with it and bounce back and apply the learnings in future, the sooner you can move on and get back to be on top of your game."

IT'S NOT EASY TO REMAIN IN FLOW, BUT IT'S WORTH FIGHTING FOR

What do you think is worth fighting for, and what's your definition of fighting? To me, positive things I can achieve in life and in business are what's worth fighting for. Starting a new life in Australia at the age of 44 wasn't a logical or easy move, but it was definitely worth fighting for. Reinventing myself again and investing in myself, going from having my own company for eight years in the Netherlands to being employed again with a much lower salary than I was used to, and having to recover from the sailing accident with a severe concussion—yes, definitely worth fighting for. Getting my first job here in Australia, building a new business network, getting to know the markets and then setting up my own company again after about four years in Australia and being certified as a coach all over again—yes, very much worth fighting for. Living and working in Australia, I feel I'm the happiest and best version of myself here and I wouldn't want to change it for the world. What did it take?

Self-belief, perseverance, being focused all the time on my goals and dreams, fine-tuning along the way, and humour to keep it light and see the absurdity of situations when needed. And yes, ignoring those who said I couldn't make it. Because yes, before I left, some people told me that at my age, nobody would be waiting for me here.

When it's worth fighting for, it's usually about how you can be most effective and get there soonest. If something is hard to achieve or against the odds, and you know you really want this, then being as effective you can be makes sense—you know there will be hurdles to get there.

How can you get there by thriving and not by surviving? "Fighting" to get there consists of doing absolutely everything to figure out what the best way to get there is and taking a step back before you start with action. The first step: Utilising the Scenario Thinking Framework™—keep finetuning along the way and never give up. But achieving what you are fighting for will be your reward. That's what I mean when I say, "Isn't it worth fighting for?" Any change for the better, requires continuous action.

Other "worth fighting for" situations could be your dream job, creating a high-performance team, getting a certain project off the ground, launching a new program, getting buy-in, closing a deal, running that marathon, climb that mountain, etc. If we don't have dreams and we don't set ourselves goals, then what's the point? Achieving those dreams and goals requires action but—depending on your own DNA makeup and your awareness of it—you can tailor your approach to the most suitable, challenging and rewarding way. Keep pushing yourself for what you think is worthwhile, interesting, exciting, meaningful and beneficial to improve people's lives.

Here are two encouraging quotes I like to share:

"Many of life's failures are people who did not realise how close they were to success when they gave up."—Thomas Edison, American inventor—in fields like electric power generation, mass communication and sound recording—and business man, who has been described as America's greatest inventor. He too faced adversity, as he was made to believe he was too stupid to learn, but it seemed he had dyslexia. Imagine if he had given up after his first failures.

And: "It takes 20 years to build a reputation and five minutes to ruin it. If you think about that, you'll do things differently." —Warren Buffett, CEO at Berkshire Hathaway, American business magnate, investor, speaker and philanthropist and one of the world's wealthiest men, with a net worth of 85 billion USD at 88 years.

We only have one life and, as we all know, life is short. And I believe it's what you make of it. Think about world-famous physicist Stephen Hawkins, who achieved so much and left behind an amazing legacy—making discoveries about the black hole and radiation, publishing leading scientific books, receiving the highest honours—and yet his disease, a rare early-onset slow-progressing form of motor neurone disease that destroyed his ability to move and speak without mechanical assistance, appears to be a profound, almost insurmountable, obstacle, because of his condition. I think he was and still is truly inspiring. As we get older and more seasoned in our roles, many leaders like to share knowledge, empower others, and enrich or better the lives of others. Think about how you, as a leader, can bring about meaningful change. What do you love doing? What are you good at? What would your purpose be, which gives you fun and fulfilment while doing it? It makes your week so much more interesting if you are driven by that, rather than that by a pay-check, your pension or your mortgage payments.

Can I hear you making excuses about why you can't try to fight for something or how you don't know what's worth fighting for? Sometimes, following your heart and contributing to what you value most comes with sacrifice or compromise, but isn't that worth fighting for in the end?

When I entered into the full-on, sailing challenge, The Round Britain and Ireland Race, in 2003, racing two weeks nonstop against the prevailing wind and currents, with no showers, decent sleep or decent food, it wasn't all fun and games—it was tough, cold, scary, and full of challenges such as being seasick for the first three days, dealing with unknown situations, aligning myself with others, contributing to the team (crew) work, and persevering. But, boy, was it worth it. All the learnings, getting to know myself better, learning how to be more effective, learning from others, learning how to deal with setbacks and adversity, and then getting a warm welcome on our return to Southampton port and a shiny trophy on top of it—priceless. And now, 15 years later, I'm still enjoying and using those insights to my benefit.

When are you in peak performance or flow state? When do you forget the time because you feel like you're on to something good, or in flow with your team? When do you see an opportunity to improve something, or an opportunity for growth or a new approach? Think about it and make some notes to explore further, with a trusted mentor or friend as a sounding board. You'll surprise yourself with what it means to you and how addicted you get to it. It's contagious. As a leader, this is where you will build your leadership and empower your team.

When we are faced with challenges or adversity, we can feel vulnerable or don't immediately see ways to deal with it. We all make excuses at first. But it's how quickly you can turn it around and say, "You know what? I will not let this define me, I want to come out stronger." When you're old, you'll only regret what you didn't do.

HOW PROACTIVE DECISION MAKING (AND SCENARIO THINKING™) HELPS MANAGE AND MAINTAIN YOUR PEAK PERFORMANCE

What do I mean by "proactive decision making"? As a leader, you need to make so many decisions throughout the day that it can be daunting. But procrastination or reactive decision-making doesn't always pan out in your (team's) best interest. Proactive decision making helps you to stay more in the driver's seat.

This article describes it really well: "How to Make Proactive Decisions by Cynthia Measom," "If you are active rather than passive in the workplace or if you take the initiative to prepare for events rather than react to them, you are likely a proactive decision-maker"

That's what the Scenario Thinking Framework™ is all about: To get into action and tackle an issue head on, demonstrating proactive behaviour, and look at how the desired or future situation ideally would look like. Then anticipate, prepare and design next steps to get there. Knowing how to ask for help or utilise and empower your team, tapping into your strengths, is what will make you successful.

HOW CAN THE SCENARIO THINKING FRAMEWORK™ HELP?

The Scenario Thinking Framework™ seems like such a simple tool and, in principle, it is. Using the framework will increase your adaptability and your proactive decision-making skills—you are actively designing a scenario for yourself to take the next step. However, there are some complex elements you need to take into consideration. It's what makes it worthwhile, but at the same time makes you understand why it needs self-awareness of your DNA makeup and lots of practice to get it in your muscle. When you look at the process flow and the elements of the Scenario Thinking Framework™ (as outlined in Chapter 2), you'll see that you have to do the work to come up with your best scenario for decision making, coping and winning strategies. You'll use introspection, self-reflection, knowledge of which strengths and values you have and can utilise, and knowledge of what's important/meaningful for you. Without that, it's more of a guessing game. You will also deal with assumptions, beliefs, habits and how to make them work (better) for you. With no self-awareness and willingness to do the work on these topics, this is not the tool for you. It doesn't mean you need to make a study out of it, but it means you need to raise your awareness of what you're made of, so that you know which buttons to push best, in which situations. Furthermore, you need to convince yourself first if you want to get the best out of yourself and your team and be most effective. That's when you can start using the tool to your advantage.

Pro-activeness is anticipating and preparing yourself proactively for a challenging or difficult conversation, meeting or other situation you need to deal with. Rather than wait and see and then react to that situation, you might like to be ahead of the game and make sure that, by anticipating and preparing your best scenario, you can have a more effective conversation or meeting. You'll have more control and influence over a situation when you do prepare. You will be less likely to experience a high level of stress when things don't go your way, and therefore you will be able to remain calm and listen more deeply, improvise and be creative with coming up with a new approach then and there.

Peak performance, as you may remember, requires a healthy dose of stress. This means that you need just enough stress to keep you alert and get creative, but not so much that it stresses you out. Everyone needs to figure out for themselves where that tipping point is. But if you know yourself, when you see that you start to shift from having a good dose of stress to getting stressed out, that's your cue to take a step back and change your approach. Pushing through will only cement the Struggle state that you are in, which is exhausting. What I usually do, and I know others do too, is to get inspiration: I talk with someone I trust and admire about how they make decisions, or I read (a lot) about how other people have achieved their goals, or I do something totally unrelated to clear my mind, like going for a walk. Basically, you need to stop doing what you're doing, relax your mind and figure out what you could do instead. Make this world a better place and start with yourself. That's always the best place to start.

A coachee I worked with who was more a high achiever than a high performer and needed buy-in for a restructure of a big part of the company, which would save costs and gain efficiency. He proactively used the Scenario Thinking Framework™ every step of the way. What

I noticed when he was using it was that he gained confidence in his decision-making abilities, he got more joy out of consulting his peers and he had a smoother buy-in because he included his peers in his train of thought. They told him they felt more respected and listened to. My coachee mentioned to me that he felt more creative with all the buy-in and contributions for his approach from his peers and his responsibilities now felt more like a mission than a chore.

Being proactive and using the Scenario Thinking Framework™ helps prevent procrastination, struggling, postponing making decisions, ignoring dilemmas, etc. The impact of not being proactive can force you deep into Struggle state where you're not being as effective, not progressing and are demotivating people around you. It's exhausting and stressful, and the competition will pass you by. At some point it's a standstill. Every contribution counts. Don't hold back on your ideas— discuss them, brainstorm, read, learn, finetune and go for it. Now you know how.

Decision making is hard enough when you have a day full of complex issues that you need to make decisions on—let alone making proactive decisions. But proactive decision making is not as daunting as you might think. The more senior you get, the more you have to make the decisions. Make sure you do your research, weigh up your options, and let Scenario Thinking™ work for you when considering your best outcome. And don't forget that you have a team of experts and peers to brainstorm with and help you prepare your proactive decisions.

High achievers might turn to proactive decision making quicker, however, high performers will be more thorough. It's a fine balance— and again, it's different in every situation. A simple example that comes to mind is of a coachee I worked with from a multinational company who was too thorough. He told me that his lack of proactive decision making had cost him a promotion, and he now wanted to improve his decision-making skills. The year before he was pressured to make a new, essential hire as the team's workload was too high and mistakes were being made.

My coachee was prone to let his perfectionism get in the way and, instead of directly hiring the candidate who seemed qualified for the job when he found him, he decided to interview two more candidates to make sure he had chosen the right one. This process took longer than he hoped for, and his first candidate found another job. So now he was forced to choose between the two other candidates, and they needed more guidance and training than he could afford. He got stuck in the operational side of things, which made his boss pick his peer for the desired promotion. He was told by his boss that he didn't see enough proactive decision making from him, and thus wasn't convinced he was ready for the senior leadership role.

You don't want to end up with others deciding for you, so use the Scenario Thinking Framework™ as your go-to tool. It's free and it helps in any situation where you'd like to be in the driver's seat. While using the Scenario Thinking Framework™, try to be proactive with your decision making from the current to the desired state. You're in a leadership role for a reason.

The "normal" way of working, processes, bureaucracy, red tape in big corporates, big teams, many peers and stakeholders, all might delay fast decision making, but the better you anticipate and prepare, the more proactive you'll be and the easier you'll get buy-in when you're ahead with your thinking and your research.

CHAPTER CONCLUSION

Managing and maintaining your peak performance or flow state is never an easy feat. Elite athletes and leaders alike will go through all the states. We're all human and we all face adversity. But again, it's how you deal with it, and knowing how to deal with it for your DNA make up, is what helps or hinders you. When you get better at something, would you like to go back to the level you were at before? Not likely, right? —not now you can see the benefits of working more effectively and being able to achieve the goals you set out to do. And when we figure out how our level of high performance works for us, it's easier to help others to get there too.

Knowing what you're made of helps tremendously in shifting states. Only you know what makes something worth fighting for. Don't let self-doubt creep in. There's always a solution. Just start now, take it step by step and make it your priority. It will save you time later. Wouldn't you like to make that "fight" as effective and time-efficient as possible, using a process of which you know the steps to take? Keep practicing your proactive decision making using the Scenario Thinking Framework™, implement it daily and help others who are doing it too. Let it surprise you with what you're capable of.

THE IMPORTANCE OF KEEPING THE OVERVIEW AND KNOWING WHEN TO RESET

This chapter provides some practical approaches helping you to expand your toolbox. The key for leaders to thrive in adversity and especially in a fast-paced ever-changing world, is to know how to keep the overview and to reset regularly. Everyone, even the best leaders, can sometimes feel a bit overwhelmed with competing priorities and demands, or by focussing too long on something. They can get stuck in the day-to-day, the operational side of the business, temporarily ignoring their strategic direction or the bigger picture.

To avoid getting stuck in the operational mire for too long, you must prioritise the bigger picture first. Without the bigger picture, it's hard to know your direction. You can't always be your best, at your peak performance. Sometimes adversity hits us from several sides at once. Wouldn't it be great if you could then still stay on track and stay focused?

In Chapter 4, we spoke about leaders being high achievers and high performers. High achievers can be obsessed or are laser-focused about achieving their goals. They're prone to taking off on their own and not including other people and making them part of their train of thought. High performers are more effective and sustainable in their approach and keep working on the buy-in they got whilst moving forward. Let's have a look at when it's time to press pause for these high achievers and high performers, to take a step back, regain the overview, set priorities and hit the reset button, to remain productive and contributing to the bigger picture.

HOPE IS NOT A STRATEGY: ACT

Just keeping the boat afloat in a storm and hoping to arrive at your destination is the same as saying, "I hope this will work." Hope is not a strategy. Action is. You must act for better outcomes, and it all starts with having the overview. It's important to adjust and reset regularly and reflect on whether the direction you're heading is still the right one. You need to know if the priorities that you and your team are working on are still the most important ones, considering the current situation, or whether you need to finetune.

At some point, everyone is dealing with how to get back on track. From my coachees, I often hear the remark: "I don't have time and headspace for strategic thinking." Although they know they have to remind themselves of the bigger picture and the overview, they don't make it their priority. However, when they do prioritise it, they also report being clearer on direction and priorities, which makes it easier to delegate. Then everything falls more into place.

We all have high workloads and, in my world, if it becomes complex and there are a lot of competing priorities, it never works to just push through without stepping back and thinking, "How can I work smarter? How can I get better organised? What are my top three priorities?" That's why I came up with an overview that works for you.

WHAT DOES THE OVERVIEW LOOK LIKE?

Your overview will be most effective if your most important priorities like project and workflow data, and their timeline, are all in one place. Knowing how your team is tracking on the projects and workflow, in terms of milestones, due dates and professional development, will help set priorities and allocate and delegate work. Working with several hard copy post-its and notebooks, next to a to-do list on your laptop—which a lot of leaders do—means the information is scattered and you're less effective as a result. You literally can't see the overview in one glance. No wonder you can lose sight of the bigger picture.

To give you an example, a coachee I worked with was a director in an international organisation. She had a rather large span of control. About seven people reported directly to her and another hundred or so reported to those people. So, you can imagine that she had enough on her plate. When I asked her how she kept the overview, she showed me that she had three different to-do lists, project and team lists using different tools. She mentioned that in her weekly one-on-ones with her direct reports, she had a hard time shifting gears and guiding them in their priorities and delegating the right tasks to them. You can imagine that if you have to look up your priorities and tracking your teams' progress from different lists and documents, and can't see them clearly in front of you, it can give you some anxiety and a feeling of being disorganised at some point. If you are trying to memorise it all you might forget something, but it's for sure taking up headspace and energy that can be used more productively. So, for example, she would show up going from one meeting to the next, without having the overview. Each time she had to take time to gather her thoughts again, reminding herself of the last update and developments and where she and her team needed to take next steps. She was not on top of things. This approach made it very hard to structure and articulate her thoughts properly or contribute in a clear way to her peers in a meeting, especially having to chair the meeting. When we worked through that, she realised that the lack of having one good overview was not doing her any favours. Usually it takes a couple of tries for people to get to one that works for them.

I'm not talking about a to-do list, but about the strategic priorities and project or activity flow of yourself and your team to drive your business. In the overview that I usually use, the main features are a timeline horizontally at the top of the document and the priorities and projects on the lefts side vertically. It's about seeing in one glance how your time is allocated, how you drive your projects and workflow, and which time slots you can still use when you need to do something urgent or unexpected. The easiest type of document is an Excel spreadsheet (see the illustration on page 109), where you can then add several tabs. The main tab functions as the general overview to start with. On the other tabs, you can allocate your individual team members and track their individual projects, milestones and development needs. And you can also have a tab for your stakeholders and one to track your own milestones and development needs. Keeping the document updated by inserting just a couple of keywords/notes daily will give you an overview that will come alive and speak to you. This will allow you to much more quickly realise where you should put your focus and energy. And you will save time and energy in return.

TIMELINE PRIORITIES	OWNERSHIP	March	April	May	June	EOFY	July	August
PROJECTS	column to note owners of project	keywords/ colours/due date	keywords/ colours/due date	keywords/ colours/due date	keywords/ colours/due date	Reflection notes	keywords/ colours/due date	keywords/ colours/due date
Project 1								
Project 2								
Project 3								
New ideas in progress								

Example of basic, empty overview Excel.
See page 119 for example of a detailed, filled in overview.

So now you know what I mean with having the overview, how do you know you need to regain the overview and reset? I will help you recognise the signs that you need to reset. Then, what are the risks of not having the overview and the perks of having the overview? And finally, you'll learn the best ways to reflect and reset.

WHAT ARE THE SIGNS THAT A RESET IS DUE?

Before you can regain the overview, you must identify the signs that you need to take a step back, set a new direction, or have a rest. Being on top of things requires resilience. Most people believe that we need to be tough and have grit, which usually shows up in the form of pushing ourselves to make one more call, having one more meeting, facilitate one more workshop—all whilst we are not at our best, not in flow and are craving some rest. You might tell yourself you are tough, and you just need to go on to be successful, but you're actually not so productive anymore. These signs appear just before exhaustion sets in, and you find yourself unable to respond creatively to other people's ideas or remarks. It shows up when you get too reactive or too impulsive in what you're about to say. Somebody might give you feedback, and you react defensively, or you are annoyed or bored with the topic and you don't have a poker face. Chances are that whatever your reply will be, it will not be received well.

That's a sure sign that you need to reset. But why wait so long? The lack of a recovery period is very much in the way of our ability to be resilient and successful. According to an article in *HBR*, "Resilience is about how you recharge and not how you endure" by Shawn AnchorMichelle Gielan June 24, 2016, there is a direct scientific correlation between lack of recovery and increased incidence of health and safety problems. I don't know about you, but I tend to do and say a lot of things from my intuition. But, as the article describes, "homeostasis" is actually a thing. It's a fundamental biological concept which describes the ability of the brain to continuously restore and sustain wellbeing. "When the body is out of alignment from overworking, we waste a vast amount of mental and physical resources trying to return to balance before we can move forward." Author Arianna Huffington describes in her book *The Sleep Revolution* that "sacrificing sleep for the sake of productivity actually leads to 11 days lost productivity per year per worker, or about $2,280." You can imagine how this will add up for a company, or for a city or a country. The New York Times bestselling authors Jim Loehr and Tony Schwartz, have contributed to this topic in their book *The power of full engagement: Managing energy, not time, is the key to high performance and personal renewal* by stating that "if you spend too much time in the performance zone, you need more time in the recovery zone, otherwise you risk burnout." Your brain doesn't stop working when you are on the couch at home at night checking your phone constantly, whilst you should be recovering. Or when you keep going over the day thinking of ways to do things better, anticipate decisions you need to make or just writing some more emails to have a head start for the next day. We all know the feeling that when you then finally go to bed, your brain has a hard time switching off and you find yourself still awake in the middle of the night. That's why I strongly believe that you must be resetting regularly during your day, and recovering multiple times during your day to actually build and manage your resilience. This means giving your body and your brain a rest. When you reset on a regular basis it becomes a habit to do so, and ultimately doesn't require much of your time.

In his article "Say goodbye to stress: How to recognise burnout symptoms before it's too late" Tony Robbins says it really simple and clear: "Our health is the most valuable resource we have." The thing is when you are close to burnout and showing burnout symptoms more than not, it doesn't just affect you, but also the people around you. Your relationships in the workplace and in your personal life will very much be impacted by our stress. Specifically, in your role as a leader trying to role model the right, productive behaviours for your team. Signs that you might be heading for a burnout show up as making careless mistakes, not having energy to contribute in a positive way, memory loss, headaches, a cold that proves hard to recover from, sleep deprivation, taking things personally, not being able to keep your composure and snapping at people, losing your train of thought a lot, and more serious health issues like premature ageing and getting yourself in accidents. Those are all sure signs that you most probably pushed it too far or have struggled for too long. It is hard to ask people for help but consider the above and ask yourself why you shouldn't.

There are two kinds of reset. A hard reset is more about a deep reflection on your life and your routines. A soft reset, where you step back and take some rest, ranging from just stepping away from your desk for a walk around the block, to doing mindfulness or exercise and not checking your phone for a while, is what we're talking about here.

LIFE IS MORE THAN JUST WORK

We're humans, not robots. There's more to life than just work. For a high-profile job with massive workload and dynamics, it's imperative to set priorities and find balance. I always tell my coachees who struggle: "Health and family first, then work." Because if you don't do it in that order, then life gets in the way—literally. A hard reset is the only cure for going down that path.

In both hard and soft resets, it's our physical and mental wellbeing that allow us to peak and to thrive. You need to take your wellbeing seriously. As a leader, you're a role model. Through your behaviour and how you show up, you're setting an example of a way of working, so you need to be extra mindful of that.

I once worked with a coachee who was quite overwhelmed with her mounting workload and she told me she didn't have time to reset. It was only during our coaching sessions that she finally relaxed and took time for reflection. In her everyday life, having three kids and a high-profile job, family and friend commitments, she found herself unable to relax. However, when she relaxed in our session and started thinking, she also got emotional being aware that she hardly allows any self-care and that she should do that more often. She had just been promoted a couple of weeks ago—and that's why we were working together, to provide a smoother transition. There were a couple of big, prestigious projects that she needed to get off the ground, so a lot of priorities were competing for her attention and she had to manage a big team as well.

She was quite a perfectionist. While wanting to do well at work, she also wanted to be a role model for her direct reports as well as for her kids. But when I first met her, she was exhausted, not in her best form, rushed, a bit moody, not creative and not effective. Through our sessions, she would break down in front of my eyes when I simply asked her if her situation was working for her. She acknowledged a heartfelt "no," and then we started to discuss what we needed to change for her and what that would look like. She had lost track of what really mattered to her and lost her sense of purpose. She described waking up in the morning unable to find her enthusiasm to go to work because of her exhaustion and the stress that it caused. She needed to reset. If your focus and purpose are not aligned, you need to ask yourself if it's worth it. All this exhaustion comes with a cost and it's not sustainable to keep this up.

YOUR RESET DIAGNOSTIC: QUESTIONS TO ASK YOURSELF

My coachee, it seemed, needed to reset. Asking yourself why you are pushing yourself so hard and what the costs are is a start. As Simon Sinek, well-known author, thought leader and speaker always states: "Start with why." Not knowing what motivates you and what you're working towards, can only get you so far.

You might think, perhaps my coachee just wasn't suitable for the role. If that is the case, why was she promoted? One of the reasons she was told, was that they saw the growth potential and she was a great communicator upwards and sideways. But she had a lot to deal with both personally and at work. She had change, disruption, restructure of the organisation, and looming deadlines for the projects she was responsible for. By regaining the overview and resetting, she re-energised, and the enthusiasm she lost when previously trying to achieve goals with her team came back again. After a reset and a short break, she regained her sense of purpose.

A reset is nothing dramatic, and it doesn't need to be a big time-consuming process either. Resetting regularly during your day, stepping away from your desk, changing up activities, hydrating yourself with drinking water and having your lunch and nutritious snacks at regular times, will allow you to see things more clearly with more headspace for creative thinking. You will start having the overview again and start seeing where you have time slots left to do some strategic thinking.

Most people enjoy the reflection and are happy with a soft reset. They tend to do it more often once they've experienced it. Sometimes, though, the exhaustion has been going on for too long. They might be at the brink of a nervous breakdown. They're not at their best, and that's when they might need a hard reset. That's usually when they must take a longer time off and regroup.

To gauge for yourself whether you need to reset, ask yourself these questions about your state of mind:

- Is this situation still working for you?
- Are you in a state of utter exhaustion where you doubt yourself or lack confidence?
- What values do you have that are being compromised?
- What is happening now? Is that different from the goals you had for yourself?
- When you hear yourself answering this question, what do you think about what you have just said? When people say it out loud, it can be very confronting

Ask yourself these questions about your physical health:
- Have you worked through all your breaks today?
- Have you eaten anything?
- How many coffees have you had?
- Are you dehydrated?
- Are you sleeping well?

Answer these questions and see how you're scoring. A combination of physical and mental signs can contribute to you needing a reset.

WHAT ARE THE RISKS OF NOT HAVING THE OVERVIEW?

There are several risks if you do not regain the overview. You might lose to the competition—they might be more agile and quicker at getting products to market because you haven't seen a number of signs. You might risk disengagement of your team—you have a high turnover of people because people who don't have the overview and work on the detail are prone to be quite self-absorbed. They focus on their work rather than having a peripheral view and knowing what's going on in their team and with their peers. Peripheral vision in general is the ability to see objects and movements outside of the direct line of vision, which helps to not become tunnel visioned. Keep looking around you and prioritise what aligns with the strategy.

When you have the overview, it makes you more creative and effective because you have more space to think and to have ideas. You're using a different part of the brain—operating in a more spacious way, away from the pressure. When the pressure rises it affects how we handle our workload, conflicts and our relationships. It can lastingly alter our brains. How you handle difficult situations can impact your mood, memory and even your lifespan. Read more in the article by *Psychology Today* from 6 April 2011: "Under Pressure: your brain on conflict" on how cortisol, which is released in our brain when under stress, affects our memories.

One of my favourite books is *The Leading Brain* by Friederike Fabritius. I highly recommend reading it. She talks about how, when you're too stressed, those primary tendencies come up from your brain and you go into fight or flight mode. Everything is a threat to your brain in that state and you need to reset yourself. Feeling threatened doesn't make you creative or productive. You'll likely go on the defence, react impulsively or make emotional decisions versus well thought out logical conclusions.

Another useful tool in this context is the SCARF model—created by Dr. David Rock, Director of the NeuroLeadership Institute—which uses neuroscience to effectively lead and work with others. The Scarf model is particularly useful to read about when you are interested in how this brain-based model helps us to understand about collaboration and people's behaviours and how to influence them.

To use a different perspective, I'm sure that by now a lot of people have heard of Marie Kondo and her show on Netflix and her books, *The Life-Changing Magic of Tidying Up* and *Spark Joy*. The first time I watched her show, I had just moved to a new house and I got rid of six garbage bags, both before and after the move, so I definitely related to that. What Marie Kondo claims is that you should only hang onto things that bring you joy. I feel that when people are under a lot of stress and they don't have the overview anymore, they don't feel the joy or fulfilment anymore, and that negatively affects them. So that's when you have to ask yourself: What am I doing? Is this still worth it? Is this still working for me?

When you declutter your house according to Marie Kondo's techniques, you have a better overview of what you own and where everything belongs. You know where to find things. You have more space to put things and you can finally walk through your home without stumbling over things. It's the same in business. It will be easier for you to make decisions and to delegate because you have more headspace and you know better where you're going.

Last but not least, mentioning self-management here is of the essence. In a Huffington Post article "Leading by Example: A Guide to Self-Management" written by Founder and Chief Leadership Officer of Blueprint Leadership, Diane Kucala, self-management is described as "an individual demonstrating self-control and an ability to manage time, priorities and decision-making capacity, creating a more effective leadership style." To my point, when we lose the overview and we are due to reset, self-management needs to be top of mind. We don't show up as our best selves when we are exhausted, disorganised, stressed, and being too reactive or defensive in our responses. In meetings where the pressure is on, it's hard to keep your composure and the ability to think on your feet, think creatively and productively. Looking for outcomes that benefit all might even become an impossible task.

Next to self-control, Diane mentions other critical elements of self-management that benefit best outcomes: Productivity, authenticity, adaptability to change and initiative. All these great abilities suffer when we are under too much pressure. I agree with the author that "to successfully lead an organisation, you must be willing to initiate self-management in all aspects of managing others, understand your strengths and weaknesses and maintain responsibility for your actions." As a leader, you are a role model and your behaviour will rub off on your team. The better you are at self-management, the more you can empower your team and let them practice their own self-management and drive best outcomes.

PRIORITISE A RESET, IT WILL SAVE YOU TIME

You're probably thinking, "This is all very well, but how do I get there? I don't have time for this." People say that to me often. They might see or recognise the signs, but they don't see when they should give it attention. My answer is that you need to prioritise it instead of waiting until you don't have a choice to deal with it. The time you spend on regaining the overview will create more time in your schedule. When you take a step back and reflect on where you need to go (which really doesn't need to take long, especially when you do it regularly), and step out of the operational, you will have the time that you're craving.

All of us have this moment where we get completely caught up in the busy world. We all do this. Sometimes we do it because we feel more comfortable being busy than grappling with the challenges of stepping back and having a look at the overview. Maybe we have a self-limiting belief about how good we are at our job, or maybe you keep comparing yourself to your peers who seem to have it all without much effort. No matter what our situation, we all need to learn to take a step back.

If you ignore or neglect the signs, if you're in denial, or if you have that lack of self-knowledge or self-awareness, when these signs show up you might end up in more trouble than getting on top of your game. So, if you find it hard to reset regularly on your own, start blocking times in your calendar to remind yourself and be ahead of the game. Ask a peer or a friend to keep you accountable when you show up unproductive or reactive. Asking for help when you sense you're not on top of your game is not a bad idea or a sign of weakness, it shows humility: no one can do everything by themselves, and people usually enjoy supporting one another and achieving outcomes together.

THE PERKS OF HAVING THE OVERVIEW

You have read about several perks throughout this chapter. To recap, an overview will allow you to move faster between priorities. Having the bigger picture will make it more compelling, especially if it's to the point. It comes with setting strategic and bigger operational priorities. When you use your overview well, you'll get better at time management, delegate better and empower your team more with ownership or autonomy. They will start to think for themselves. For everyone, it gives a healthy sense of urgency. It allows for more strategic headspace and you anticipate future events and adversity better.

A perfect example is a coachee who I worked with. He was having trouble with delegating to his team and keeping them accountable. Because he felt he couldn't delegate or wait around to explain things to them, he thought he had to carry out the tasks himself, keeping to a tight deadline. His own priorities were then compromised, and he had to work late more and more. This went on for weeks. We started to create an overview for him to use and he was surprised by how easy it was and how little maintenance it needed.

Most leaders I work with will shift from having multiple overviews to the one. It's different for everyone. It's tailored to the person and it allows them to see their own priorities on the timeline.

I once worked with somebody who was a great leader, but he was chaotic in organising and always keen to get going without too much thinking or consideration. He had great industry knowledge and he was somebody who always came up with ideas to engage and enthuse everyone. But his project and his team were not on track because he was so all over the place with his ideas. For him, having the overview allowed him to delegate more clearly and assign relevant things to his team. The team got more autonomous and he could cover more ground and make quicker progress. Because of that, he even made a promotion. He still uses that type of overview and has taught his team to use it as well.

On page 120 you can see an example of how your overview might look when keywords are used.

I have been working with this type of overview and with mind mapping tools (like iThoughts2go, which is also free) for almost my whole working life. Being a visual person, when you have that setup, it speaks to you more clearly than just having to-do lists. It really gets into your muscle because you can design or tailor your own overview and start to thrive. For me, at least, everything clicked in my head and it helps me to more effortlessly navigate a complex world.

TIMELINE	OWNERSHIP	March	April	May	June	EOFY	July	August
Priorities	column to note owners of project	keywords/colours/date	keywords/colours/date	keywords/colours/date	keywords/colours/date	Reflection notes	keywords/colours/date	keywords/colours/date
PROJECTS								
Project 1	X	delegate operational and design tasks	due date 15/4, make sure buy in from ELT before 10/4	prep team offsite presentation	team offsite			
		set up 6 months strategy as f/up		gather all team preso's etc				
Project 2	Y	presentation for team for buy in and delegation	next steps to present to ELT for input finance & marketing	finalise dual reporting system		fine-tune strategy for new year		
Project 3	X & Y	write preso synergy and layout new floor	input from Z re design	move team to 3rd floor, integrate w other department	due date EOFY, discuss f/up new year depending on success; clear old floor by 10/6			
New ideas in progress	Z	discuss and delegate for team members development	check all are having a side project for personal growth				presentations from all team embers re their business idea new year	
	red	due date						
	green	ongoing						
	yellow	something to look forward to, motivational project						
	empty box	time for 1:1's, urgent projects, strategise, etcetc						

IT'S NEVER TOO LATE TO START THIS PRODUCTIVE HABIT

I'm sure you're telling yourself you already have an—or even *the*—overview. But how often are you going through papers, your notebook or your memories, trying to look for the latest update before you go into a meeting or a performance review with one of your direct reports? Do you have one overview? By having a system that allows you to track progress and not lose information, you will then free up time. I think it would be a mistake to think you don't need or couldn't use an overview. If you do have one and maintain it regularly, congratulations. I'm sure you agree with me on the perks. Everyone could do with some help when it comes to organisation.

Check out the list of perks above again. Now think about a time when these perks would have helped you in a tough situation. Having the overview in the one place/document allows you to have all the information you need at your fingertips. If you find you're lacking in some areas, do a soft reset, take a step back and consider what steps you need to take to make yourself more efficient and fully informed. The best way to reflect and reset is to do it regularly and constantly. That's when it costs the least amount of time. Sometimes a couple of minutes is enough. And the good news is, it's never too late to start this healthy habit. You can start right now.

What lifts you up? What energises or relaxes you? These are the things you need to consider when choosing the best way for you to reflect and reset. It's so important to know what you're made of, and what your DNA makeup is.

- What are your strengths, your experience, your knowledge?
- What is important to you?
- What is your purpose, what are you working towards and who do you want to be?

When you know all that, you also know where you're going when you're in flow, and you can articulate that to your team and your peers to get buy-in. That's usually when you find the most synergy and productivity. And that usually will be when you have a good overview. Also, it prevents us from getting bored or complacent. You will keep yourself sharp and be the best you can be.

TAKING THE HURDLES TO GET TO AN OVERVIEW AND RESET

What is usually in the way to start this efficient and effective habit? Maybe not surprisingly, *we* are. You are the only person who knows when you don't have the overview and when you're struggling in being effective. People might observe you're struggling but they might be busy or struggling themselves as well. At some point you can tell something is lacking: a lack of direction, focus, rest, exercise, mindfulness, fun. Or something is in the way and that can be what we tell ourselves: What are we afraid of if we think about taking the time to reset? The fear of missing a deadline? The fear of people's perception that you can't push through? The fear of letting your team down? When anxiety, self-doubt or lack of confidence are in the way, it's very hard to just push through and get best outcomes.

Take a step back, reflect on what is not going well and what is going well. Allow yourself 10-20 minutes to take a walk, and look at your work again with fresh eyes. Pick someone's brains on where you're stuck and share your thoughts on possible next steps. Hear other perspectives, or have a casual conversation and a laugh to feel more relaxed again. Involve others in your train of thought more, is what a true high performer would do to get inspired and creative again. It's always good to talk to somebody who's got a fresh perspective when you're stuck in something.

Be honest to yourself and realistic in what you can pull off by yourself and where a team effort is better. When you balance this well, you feel like you can move mountains. Create or get back to your overview and make sure that you reset priorities and finetune to the current situation.

CHAPTER CONCLUSION

Having the overview and knowing how to reset, has so many benefits. Yes, you must invest some time in it, but you get a lot back. All it takes is about 20 minutes to create your Excel overview or a similar suitable platform and have the *one* overview, instead of multiple hard and soft copy sources. From then onwards, you can keep track of everything daily, with just a couple of minutes at a time. It's worth the investment. Daily maintenance of the overview will be such a helpful tool. You need to trust the process and learn to read the signs for yourself faster to remain on top of your game.

Leaders sometimes think they have the overview, but getting your information and updates from five different sources is really wasting valuable time. What is the importance of "having the overview"? As a leader, you're not an individual contributor who's task-oriented. You're responsible for more than to-do tasks in your day. As a leader, you must contribute to the company's bottom line. You need to know what the company stands for and what it is you need to contribute, guiding your team to take the necessary steps to get there. That is what I mean with having the overview: knowing what the bigger picture is, knowing what to focus on, how to drive your business and how you're tracking strategically, instead of dealing with the operational stuff that needs to be done on a daily basis.

How do you know as a leader that you're contributing to the bottom line of the company? It's about not being stuck in detail, being able to see a big picture of where things are going—who's doing well or not well, whether the operations are on track—rather than being stuck in the minutiae of who's done what, when and why.

You must remain flexible because, especially with adversity, we need to be able to know what to focus on. Having the overview increases your adaptability. As a leader with the bigger picture in mind, you need to be able to adapt when hurdles or setbacks are coming your way. If you're stuck in the operational, you don't have that. You may not even see them coming. I hope that now you know how to set up an overview, you will implement it. It saves so much time and it will make you much more effective while increasing your mental and physical wellbeing. Burnout is not just a word. It's a real risk of not getting things done and having to come back from a tough place.

It's often hard for people to accept that they don't have an effective overview, and to do something about it. Recognising the signs that you need to regain the overview, and the need for a reset, helps to prevent losing the overview and burnout. There are numerous risks if you don't, but the perks are well worth it. Overcome the hurdles, ask for help and just do it: start today, you will not regret it.

STRENGTHS MANAGEMENT

HOW TO AVOID OVERUSE OR UNDERUSE OF STRENGTHS?

This chapter is about strengths management, which is using your strengths in the most authentic, effective and balanced way. And knowing how to avoid or correct overuse or underuse of one or more of your strengths. Whether you overuse or underuse strengths, the result is the same in the sense that you're not as effective as you can be to achieve a certain outcome or response. In this chapter, I'll explain about strengths management and strengths-based coaching and the tools involved. We'll look at what typical strengths are and how to use them in a balanced way, knowing which strengths to use more or less, tailored to the situation.

By managing your strengths well as a leader, you will be far more effective in positioning yourself, being more authentic (true to yourself) with increased adaptability, confidence and resilience. After reading this chapter, you'll be more aware of how to be proactive and creative in using your strengths and improving your communication and decision making.

Knowing how to make the best use of your strengths will increase your self-awareness and it will decrease the gap between the perception you have of yourself and that others have of you. When you don't get the response you were looking for, it usually has to do with not having communicated your intentions well, your message didn't come across well and you probably haven't made the right use of your strengths. Self-awareness of how you are perceived and how you use or manage your strengths is important, so that you know which buttons to push if you need to readjust yourself.

Especially when we deal with adversity, strengths management will help to turn it to your advantage. It's a great opportunity to make adversity work for you and have fun while doing it.

STRENGTHS MANAGEMENT IS A BALANCING ACT

As a leader, you're trying to be the best you can be. It's about finding that balance where your outcomes are optimal, and your performance is effortless and authentic, because that's when you're playing to your strengths. When you overuse or underuse your strengths, it takes more effort and energy to get things right.

When you don't have the balance right it starts to fuel your limited self-belief or self-doubt—you can be overusing your strengths being overly courageous or unrealistic, or you might be underusing them, being fearful and letting others overstep your boundaries in a situation. When you're out of balance, it's important to get it back in balance and be effective once more. We are only human, so like with flow or peak performance: you can't be in that balanced state all the time. Just as we go in and out of those states, we move from balance to imbalance in strengths management, but the trick is to recognise when our strengths are not applied in a balanced way, and to know how to adapt.

Later in this chapter, I'll explain in more detail what overuse or underuse of strengths is, and how we may be doing it without even noticing. In terms of leadership, it's important to recognise this because—and I've mentioned it before—as a leader you are a role model and you are demonstrating behaviours and a certain use of your strengths that your team will pick up. And the leaders in a leadership team are even setting the organisation's culture together, by their behaviours, so it's relevant to be aware of. It requires self-knowledge and self-management to role model the best and most effective behaviours that you can.

This chapter is not about comparing your strengths to others, or a competition of who's got the best strengths. Every person is unique with their own DNA makeup of strengths. Don't compare yourself to others and the way they do things. It might not work for you. With strengths management, you can find your own authentic way of utilising your strengths to the fullest. When you self-manage, you're basically more in control of your mind and that is the best way to get into your peak performance (see Chapter 4).

In these times of constant change, we need to adapt regularly. Strengths management done well results in a balanced approach to life and to leadership, especially when you have a growth mindset. When you don't know your strengths well, or when you fall back on old habits or autopilot, you can easily fall into the trap of overusing/underusing your strengths, which might not have the outcome you were working towards.

CAN YOU BE TOO GOOD AT LISTENING, OVERUSING ONE OF YOUR STRENGTHS?

A coachee I worked with was good at listening to and understanding other people's views and at stepping into the other person's shoes. His benevolence and generosity, both strengths of his, helped in certain situations like showing consideration and kindness when someone was overwhelmed. The downside or overuse of this strength was that he let people overstep his boundaries time and time again, because he could be too selfless and generously gave space to the other person. One of his peers made decisions that impacted him and his team, but which weren't right for him and what they were working towards. And it didn't happen once. His peer consistently served their own goal with no consideration for or consulting with my coachee. Obviously, this is a typical situation to act, remember: "Only accept the status quo that's right for you." My coachee had that gut feeling but was concerned to disrupt the working relationship and was also busy with other priorities.

We started working on adjusting his approach to being more proactive and setting clearer boundaries. To do that, he had to tap into his *courage* which was also one of his strengths. He was underusing his courage while overusing his empathy and listening strengths, and he needed to be aware of that. As a first step, he initiated a conversation with his peer and shared his intention and where he needed to go. This resulted in explaining the needs of his team better as well. He also listened more deeply to his peer, seeking to understand better, and was able to think more creatively. He made suggestions that could work for them both, whilst setting his boundaries. He got a better response when he tapped more into his courage. Before all of this, he was afraid to upset the other person because of his limiting belief that he couldn't influence the situation. And his habit was to then just let it go.

Next up, I'll explain what strength-based coaching is, and how that helps with strengths management. We'll talk about what common strengths there are, and how to identify and manage your own strengths. We'll also discuss underuse and overuse, what that is and why it matters. And lastly, I'll explain how you can use the Scenario Thinking Framework™ to make changes to your approach.

HOW STRENGTH-BASED COACHING HELPS WITH STRENGTHS MANAGEMENT

As a strengths-based executive coach, I help leaders identify and use their strengths in the most effective way. That means that when they are more aware of their strengths through coaching, they will find the resources and answers they need from within, to get to the best outcomes. Strengths-based management focuses on and grows the strengths of a leader. This focus is supported by research showing that it's better to spend time, energy and money investing in and growing the strengths of employees rather than focusing on and developing their weaknesses. It doesn't mean we don't identify, or ignore, weaknesses, but we just don't dwell on them. Instead, we focus on how to be most effective using strengths more, or less, whichever the situation calls for. Also, your strengths are usually something we are good at, which applies most effortlessly and authentically and usually is fun to do and brings us joy and fulfilment.

To give you a little bit of background, a strengths-based approach that was used in social work was formally developed by a team from the University of Kansas, including Dennis Saleebey, Charles Rapp & Anne Weick. In 1997, Charles Rapp wrote *The Strengths Model*, which focused on "amplifying the well part of the patient." The popularity of his approach spread quickly and in 1999, Dr. Martin Seligman, the president of the American Psychological Association at the time, made an observation that fuelled strength-based practice:

"The most important thing we learned was that psychology was half-baked. We've baked the part about mental illness, about repair damage. The other side's unbaked, the side of strength, the side of what we're good at." Ever since, the strength-based approach has been adapted and applied to many contexts. In 1995, Marcus Buckingham and Donald Clifton introduced the strengths perspective to the business world. American, educational Psychology Professor Donald Clifton and founder of Selection Research Incorporated (SRI) helping organisations with employee selection, recruited Marcus Buckingham. After SRI acquired The Gallup Organisation in 1988, Clifton became Chairman and Gallup expanded beyond public opinion polls. It became known as a management consulting business, consulting companies on ways to improve their businesses by homing in on their employees' strengths. In 1999 Clifton created the online assessment tool Clifton StrengthsFinder (now known as CliftonStrengths) which focuses on 34 themes that make up the user's personality. More about that tool later.

People who don't usually focus on managing their strengths, tend to be more reactive in their responses. When people are under too much pressure and need to get things done, their brain freezes. They might go on autopilot and can be impulsive or stressed whilst making decisions or in their communication. Which doesn't always get the response they would like, as they haven't thought things (read: the best approach) through. As a leader who needs to deal with all sorts of dynamics and all sorts of personalities, if you don't know your own personality and you don't have a well-balanced approach then it's difficult to be the best you can be and know which strength to use more or less of. People who don't manage their strengths will not get the best outcomes that they set out to achieve.

WHAT IS STRENGTHS-BASED COACHING?

Strengths-based coaching is coaching somebody to help them manage their strengths. In my coaching practice, when the situation calls for it, we start with some sort of diagnostic—a strength-based assessment which will analyse how you see yourself, how others see you, what you're good at and how you show up in your behaviour, values, beliefs, habits, and communication. From the assessment, we then tend to focus on three to five strengths that will help my coachee if applied more effectively to situations where they need to be more resourceful.

When people start strength-based coaching, one of the immediate effects is that their confidence rises quickly. When they realise that they're good at a skill, for example developing their team, they also start to enjoy delegating more, empowering their team and getting more resourceful. Not only does doing more with that knowledge enhance your skills but it also helps the person you're impacting. It's a bit like a snowball effect. The working relationship between those people will most likely also improve.

Ever since I found out what my own strengths are, I'm always running through them in my head if I need to address a challenging or new situation. It helps to remind myself what strengths I can tap into, to address that situation in the most effective way. According to the Gallup Clifton Strengths assessment I took, my five main strengths are:

- Empathy (handy if you're a coach)
- Futuristic (helps to anticipate on future events)
- Activator (one of the most common strengths, to get something started)
- Maximiser (trying to get the most out of something)
- Discipline (handy when you're writing a book, or when you need to finish something, or to keep being self-disciplined using a specific approach)

Why did I decide to find out my strengths? I felt I was at a crossroads when I was employed within a company where the status quo didn't work for me anymore. And so, I thought, let's identify what I'm good at and let's reinvent myself again. When you go for job-interviews, you have to articulate what you're good at and what added value you can bring, especially when you are more senior. Then it's not so much about ticking all the boxes of a vacancy. I thought it might be time to have a fresh and current view on things, and so I worked with a strengths-based coach to discover my five strengths. I'm still grateful to my coach for suggesting that I go on this journey of self-discovery because it has helped me to apply my strengths better. I can now deal with any situation that, before the coaching, I would've thought was more difficult or unattainable.

Whilst I'm a coach, of course, I also have times where I can overuse or underuse my strengths, too. Nobody is perfect, right? I can be too disciplined and into my routines at times. This can make me seem inflexible to other people. I would collaborate on projects and want to work in a way that I'm used to (probably in high-achiever mode), or that I strongly believe in because I think that's the quickest way and I know I can do well. The other person might want to work in a different way, so then I have to remind myself not to be so inflexible but to think bigger picture and to step into my maximiser strength and ask, "How can I/we do that even better, making use of both our strengths?"

Going back to Chapters 3 and 4, where we talked about high achievers, high performers and peak performance, it's important to know your strengths. It allows you to feel and perform at your very best. When you are in that state, you can deal with adversity and turn it into an advantage in the most effortless way. You know how to shift from high achiever to high performer more easily. It's beneficial for both groups because they always strive for their best. When you feel that you're struggling, that is the moment, your cue. When you start procrastinating, when you get tired or your creativity is lacking, you have to take a step back and ask, "What are my strengths again?" Then you can adjust, reset and push through— as we discussed in Chapter 5—and move on.

Strength-based coaching is a research-based approach, informed by world-class practitioners, researchers, and leaders in neuroscience and psychology. It's widely used by people in a variety of fields. When

I started coaching, around 2005, people saw coaching as a way to fix somebody's shortcomings. Nowadays, it's common for leaders who have high potential, and who are rewarded with executive coaching, to do even better. Coaching has shifted over the years from a focus on weakness to focusing on strengths. I personally never use the word "weakness" or focus on it. But I believe that from the results of an assessment, you can treat *underuse* or *overuse* as what others would call a weakness. Do you need to do more of something or less of something else? And so, that is the language that I use.

This notion of strength-based leadership and therefore strength-based coaching is outlined by Ekaterina Walter in an article in Forbes in 2013, titled 'Four Essentials of Strength-Based Leadership'. Walter is a strategic business and marketing expert who has worked for various Fortune 500 brands. In this article, in which she specifically describes a strengths-based approach for teams, she describes leadership as: "Encouraging people to live up to their fullest potential and find the path they love. That, and only that will create a strong culture and sustainable levels of innovation." In using a strengths-based approach, reaching that full potential comes within reach. I believe that it works well to "do what you love, and love what you do."

Let me give you another example of what a strengths-based approach can do. I started working with a coachee a couple of years ago, who was in a leadership role, but who was still acting as a manager, more telling his team what to do and very goal- and results-oriented: very much a high achiever. But in this role, he had to be a leader, and a role model, guiding his team and empowering them to the next phase. Unfortunately, he hadn't transitioned well from manager to leader. He never had constructive and clear feedback on his performance, and, at the time, strengths assessments weren't as current as they are today. He got to where he was by doing things according to his intuition, which got him quite far but not always in an effective way. When we first met, he was a bit frustrated because his usual approach didn't work anymore, mainly because he wasn't self-aware of his strengths and how he was perceived. When we worked on that awareness, and what he could do more/less of with his identified strengths, things started to turn around.

His lack of self-awareness didn't help him to keep his composure and he wasn't focusing on building solid working relationships. He was prone to showing his frustration or impatience, which manifested in his body language, on his face and in his tone of voice. This made it harder for him to then get his point across and build those relationships he needed for buy-in. Sometimes it isn't so much that we don't know our strengths, but we're not always capable of articulating those strengths and what's happening at that moment. It's much easier if you can articulate for yourself what's happening, to then explain or share your intentions with someone else. My coachee's top strength was humour. He tended to forget this when he was under pressure. Through our coaching conversations, he was reminded that there is always a solution to any problem. By tapping into his humour he could first work on the relationship and then make his point understood. Using humour works well to make a tense situation feel lighter and it makes people feel more relaxed. It took some practice but when he finetuned his approach in an authentic way, he more effortlessly got the response he needed.

Are you thinking, "How could that help me?" When you start to identify your strengths and then articulate them for yourself and to others, that already makes you clearer and more effective in your communication about where you would like to go. You need to be able to articulate those strengths to move forward. I was one of those people who thought I knew what I was good at, but that was more of a feeling than that I was able to articulate it. The difference is, when you invest time in reflection and introspection, working with a coach, taking an assessment, getting to know the specific words to articulate your strengths, you can make people relate to you more and have a more effective and impactful conversation. Once I found my niche in executive coaching and I could articulate to people that I specialise in helping high achievers shift to high performance, enabling them through their strengths to reach peak performance more often and more effortlessly, I started to have conversations with people who were interested in that particular topic. Many examples and experiences would come up, rather than that we had a general, polite conversation about coaching. Suddenly, people recognised themselves and were keen to hear what they could do to be more effective. You connect much easier with people if they understand better what you mean. And it's easier to understand others or explain yourself if you are aware and can articulate your strengths better.

GETTING TO KNOW YOUR STRENGTHS BETTER

In the next section, I'm going to show you how to identify what your strengths are. It's a learning curve that allows you to finetune your approach but there are subtle tweaks. It's not about changing yourself, but about using your talents, your strengths, your accumulated knowledge, your experience, and your skills to do something better. And it's also about increasing your fun. Who doesn't want to do that?

You might be hesitant about trying this because you're already performing well. You might not know how to articulate your strengths and you're not the only one. Maybe it's a gut feeling around knowing what you're good at, but you don't know what strengths combination you might have and what you can do with them to increase your adaptability. I would suggest taking an assessment to find out what the gamut of your strengths is and how to amplify and share that with others.

WHAT STRENGTHS ARE THERE, AND HOW CAN I MANAGE THEM?

There are so many strengths. Leadership development organisations who have designed strengths assessments like The Leadership Circle and Gallup have perfected the articulation of strengths with their assessment tools.

Here are some examples of strengths that you may have:

- The ability to forge a caring connection
- The ability to foster team play
- Being analytical or strategic
- Being a firm decision maker
- The ability to mentor and develop others
- Having courageous authenticity
- Having a strategic focus
- Being decisive, purposeful or visionary

These are some examples of the strengths you can have. And you might have these strengths, but to use them effectively, you need to tap into those strengths more, or less. Your assessment it will highlight how others perceive your strengths and that will indicate your effectiveness in using them: are you under- or overusing them? Or you might just forget about them now and then, focusing on other strengths. Depending on your cues—usually the responses from other people—you can start to use those strengths more or less. The various assessment tools differ in the way they approach and name strengths. But it comes down to the same principle. Don't make a study of it, just pick one where the wording of the strengths appeals to you. It's more about a practical way of knowing what they mean to you and how it helps you adapt, increase your confidence, your resilience and your decision making. In my coaching practice, I usually work with my coachee's top three to five strengths and we explore how they can apply them more creatively and effectively.

When you know that you're usually good at making strategic decisions, some questions you can ask yourself to explore your strategic decision-making strength are: When you are presented with a problem, what options or perspectives do you usually come up with? Or: How do you use your strategic skills to solve a problem or make a decision? How do you contribute to the bigger picture using your strategic skills? Or: How can you tap more into your strategic skills to solve this long-term problem? How did you approach a problem in the past that had a successful outcome?

It's important to know your strengths so that you can navigate leadership more effortlessly and you know what to do more of or less of in certain situations. It helps you to explore and use your strengths to the fullest, and you can then recognise sooner when you are either overusing or underusing your strengths. That way, you can readjust, or balance the use of your strengths. This is why we call it self-management. Once you have a clear picture of your strengths, it gets easier to practice, come up with new approaches and self-manage your strengths and their application to different situations.

WHY STRENGTHS ASSESSMENTS ARE SO USEFUL

You may think you could just ask a friend what your strengths are. But I recommend you use professional assessment tools instead. They can give you an objective account of your strengths which is more helpful than one friend explaining how they see you. In business, you might have a boss, peers, direct reports and stakeholders. With a 360 degrees assessment, you have an opportunity to include all their perceptions about you on your strengths and how you use them. And nine times out of ten, your perception of yourself will probably be different from the perception that others have of you. It may not be a big gap, meaning you are quite aware of your use of strengths and effectiveness, or it may be a bigger difference than you thought. Which might help you to act in that area and become more effective. And it's the latter gap that is probably what interests you most; where you can improve your performance. It is so helpful to know that what you intend to do is not always perceived as such. Then you can act and do something about it.

In general, an assessment test can take as much as 30-40 strengths into account. When you start working with these tools, the gap between your own perception of your strengths and the perception of you from your evaluators, is a guide for what you could and want to work on. But don't focus on all the 30-something strengths, it's much better to pick three to five at the most. That way you can use your time and energy effectively by improving the use of these strengths in a focused way with a steep learning curve. And, as you know now, flow follows focus.

Also using an assessment tool is not being assessed by me as your coach, and it's not an assessment by your boss. It gives you an objective and credible third-party source to examine your strengths and to see in one glance which strengths you are using well and which strengths you can use more to be more effective, by a number of people around you. Inevitably, it can be quite challenging to see how others perceive you and your use of your strengths, but we're here to learn and grow, right?

There are many more assessments out there, but so far, as an executive coach, I prefer The Leadership Circle Profile (LCP) as it is quite rich in data. The LCP results will provide clarity on a complex mix of behavioural competencies/strengths and inner states of being. It is organised into a powerful system for understanding human behaviour and development, as well as for making sense of the interrelationships between the many dimensions being evaluated. More importantly it measures internal assumptions, as especially our habit of thought determines a great deal of our behaviour. Due to their substantial database, the assessments results also provide a benchmark to your peers' effectiveness in similar roles. By getting insights on the underlying patterns that drive behaviour, you'll gain access to new choices and possibilities. If you're interested to read more about the LCP, have a look at their website www.leadershipcircle.com. As they mention, having consciousness and competence arise together establishes high levels of effectiveness, and that's what being the best you can be is all about.

Strengths management helps you to change gears when you encounter change or adversity. Just using three strengths as a focused approach helped my coachee who didn't have great self-awareness. She was reluctant to try out new approaches, as she was under pressure and thought she couldn't afford the time for it. When we started to work on her strengths management, she was quite defensive and dismissive of any feedback.

Once she experienced the benefits of coming up with a new approach by using her strengths in a more balanced, effective way, she warmed to the idea and got more creative with it. I helped her to apply her strengths towards the written feedback, which was something that she started to enjoy when she got a better response to her new approach. She experienced that she might have the best intentions with how she showed up, but people still didn't see her as she intended. It was something she realised now she needed to work on by using her strengths better and asking more for feedback. Feedback is such a great tool to get insight about how you are perceived and realise how effective you are—or not. And asking feedback only takes around a minute, to tap someone on the shoulder. But it will save you a lot of time figuring it out for yourself.

WHY IT'S A 20-MINUTE INVESTMENT OF YOUR TIME WELL SPENT

You might be thinking, "I've already done a 360-degrees assessment and gotten feedback. I know what people think of me." That's great, but be mindful that we are evolving human beings, and hopefully your growth mindset means that you develop your strengths and effectiveness over time. So, when it's been a couple of years, make sure to redo a 360-degrees assessment to keep yourself sharp and aware. In my experience, most people don't prioritise a 360-degrees assessment for themselves or being an evaluator for others, because it takes up to 20 minutes of their day. It feels like a chore. But, boy, are they keen when the results are there. It's all about them and it explains why they are struggling or why they're performing well in certain situations, as well as how others perceive them instead of their own perceptions of themselves. Having that eye-opener makes it easier to embrace their shortcomings. They're like answers to questions that were lingering in their mind: "Why didn't I get a buy-in on a certain occasion? Why don't I seem to empower that team member? Why do I keep being stuck in the operational side of the business? However, sometimes people are not happy with the results because it can be quite confronting. But when I then emphasise strengths rather than weaknesses, and when I show them how easy it is to use your strengths more, it becomes a fun thing to do. Using this tool will help you understand your strengths and you'll be able to respond to the feedback much more effectively—and have fun while doing it.

Many companies will provide their employees with assessments, whether it's Gallup or the Leadership Circle or any other assessment tool and have a coach to do a debrief. Once debriefed, awareness is raised about what strengths they have and how they overuse and underuse them. But it's imperative not to stop there. That is where your journey begins if you want to improve yourself. To start applying your strengths in a different, more effective way, start practicing new approaches, finetune when they work or don't work for you. That's where progress starts to show.

The more senior you get as a leader, the more your role is about soft skills, optimising your behaviours and habits and how you role model them to your team and the broader organisation. The way you demonstrate these behaviours and your use of strengths will be picked up by people around you. This sets the tone for the way of working and the culture of an organisation. So, don't think that the more senior you get the less you need an assessment. The opposite is true. If you want to keep evolving keep assessing and asking for feedback regularly and keep increasing your adaptability. It's not a luxury we can do without in these fast-paced and ever-changing and complex times.

Think about which leaders you admire, or who was the best boss or manager you've had, who really motivated you. My personal example of a great boss I had was a "maximiser." It doesn't refer directly to the maximiser strength I mentioned before, but it's someone who gets the most out of you. As a high achiever, I, and so many other people, only needed a nudge to find the right direction, or where to get certain information. Just some encouragement to read something to get inspired. When I was able to ask questions and get short and clear answers back, I could move mountains. He knew me well and that worked well for me to get the best out of me. As opposed to micro management or, when asking a question, getting a lecture on a topic and you still need to find an answer to your question.

When you're in a leadership role, you're most effective when you are working in a culture where your values are aligned and where your strengths can make the most impact. When people leave a company, one of the biggest reasons is because their values are compromised. They don't feel respected or valued, or their trust is broken. Your values form the basis of your decision making. Think about it, have you ever made a good decision that goes against your own values? You might have been in a situation where someone else made a decision that impacted you and didn't align with your values. That didn't feel right, did it? Thinking of that situation, how could you use your strengths to approach that situation more effectively?

Now you are aware of your strengths, ask for more feedback. Ask your direct reports, "How do you relate to my suggestion?" Ask your peers, "What will make you agree with my train of thought?" When you start to use this open question approach, check-in with the people who you're trying to impact and effect and ask them if it's working for them. Don't use closed questions where they can say yes or no. That doesn't give you much information to adjust your approach. But ask them what works better for them, where they need extra information or guidance, etc.

At first, this process might seem a bit awkward. You might overthink it or find it too analytical. Or you might be afraid of an honest answer. You've just done all this analysing of your own strengths, and now it's time to put it into practice. The more you practice, the better you get. Part of my job is to help you practice and fin-tune in a consistent way until you get it into your muscle.

USING THE SCENARIO THINKING FRAMEWORK™ TO CHANGE YOUR APPROACH

When you know your strengths, you can combine them with the Scenario Thinking Framework™ to structure those strengths and behaviours that you want to use more effectively. You might have a challenging meeting next week, and challenging meetings or difficult conversations shouldn't be left to chance. It's good to anticipate and prepare. Stop and think about your strengths for a moment and choose a strength you can apply more effectively for that meeting. From there, things will start to fall into place, and you will show up more present and confident in the meeting.

Sometimes even subtle differences in your approach will make a huge difference to the outcome, such as changing your wording more positively or invite the other for direct feedback. For example, someone could say, "This is my opinion. (Full stop)." As you can imagine, you probably won't get a favourable response. Nor is it likely that you'll get a constructive conversation on the topic. But when you say, "I believe it should be A. What do you think?" then you have a conversation and you get feedback. This can have a massively positive effect on your outcome.

WHY USE A STRENGTHS ASSESSMENT AND THE SCENARIO THINKING FRAMEWORK™ IN COMBINATION?

As you know from Chapter 2, the Scenario Thinking Framework™ is a tool where you're not only applying your strengths for best decision-making outcomes, but it also includes the navigation around your beliefs, values, behaviours, habits, and assumptions. To use the Scenario Thinking Framework™ well, you really need to understand and be aware of your strengths and DNA makeup, for best outcomes. Not just knowing what your strengths are, but how you can use them most effectively in combination with the positive framing of your beliefs, behaviours, habits, and assumptions. This takes some practice to get in your muscle, but once it is, it only takes a couple of minutes to apply it.

A 360 degrees strengths assessment is very helpful as you have current insights on how you are perceived and how you perceive yourself regarding your leadership effectiveness. If you look at the scores on your strengths and there's a gap between those two, it often indicates that your intentions to show a certain behaviour might not be picked up by others. So, in order to become more effective, you need to adjust and try another, new approach and articulate and share your intentions or message better. This means, you need to know your DNA make up well, knowing what to make use of in that particular situation. For this new approach, the Scenario Thinking Framework™ helps you to identify which strengths to use more and helps you to anticipate, prepare and action better outcomes.

As an example, a coachee I worked with was quite surprised that she scored high on courageous authenticity, as she didn't perceive herself as courageous at all. From the written feedback her evaluators described they admired that she stood for the team, managing upwards well, championing the ideas and way of working of the team. However, my coachee found this quite normal, although challenging to do. Once she understood that her team would like to learn from her, she shared how she prepared herself for those challenging conversations and how she built her confidence to get there. And she also understood better that not everyone found it normal to have those courageous conversations. So, she started to support and empower her team more, using her strengths and beliefs and the Scenario Thinking Framework™ to do so. Most probably in the next 360, if she would keep this awareness and approach up, her perception and that of her team regarding her courageous authenticity will most likely not differ that much in scores anymore.

Sometimes after a strengths assessment, there is just the debrief on the assessment and no further follow-up. It's really a tough effort to then use that awareness and insights of the debrief by yourself going forward. As I mentioned before, after the debrief, that's when the real growth starts. I hear so often that people then just go about their usual way and don't give it another thought, and their insights fade away as they don't practice and use them. All with best intentions, but there's nobody to guide them, to hold a mirror to them to help make use and learn further from those insights.

To recognise where and how you can apply the learnings from a strengths assessment using the Scenario Thinking Framework™, practice with a coach. By using the two in combination, you have a powerful solution for challenging situations. You optimise your outcomes and you're making sure that everyone involved is part of that journey, which means you'll get the best possible outcomes. After that, you know how to adjust your approach if it needs to be more effective.

The Scenario Thinking Framework™ always surprises people with what they're capable of, and I use it to help them come up with a new approach. I'm not telling them what to do. But they think clearer when they are clear on their strengths and it takes away a lot of stress. We all know that when you have less stress you can think more clearly, more creatively. And it's easier to think more strategically and with less emotion.

CHAPTER CONCLUSION

In this chapter, we've learned all about the role of strengths in terms of leadership and that strengths can be overused or out of balance. Overusing or underusing your strengths can sometimes have a negative effect on your performance. But now, you should have the ability to recognise overuse of strengths in your own life. You can also play with your strengths more and get more creative and use them in combination with my powerful tool I introduced in Chapter 2, the Scenario Thinking Framework™.

When you take a strengths assessments, you'll find the Scenario Thinking™ tool as an add on tool to be more effective, and you will start to proactively shift from a high achiever to high performer and get into your peak performance much more easily. Picking a maximum of five strengths to focus on will give you more insight into your own capabilities, and it's simple enough to be able to implement them. When you're constantly working with your five top strengths, you'll be sure to use the best strengths to amplify your effectiveness. And you will notice that these five strengths will also enhance your other strengths as your understanding and application of them grows.

Some barriers that you might encounter when you come to really work with this strength-based approach to management, are that you might believe you can't really change your behaviour, or you'll be overly enthusiastic, cutting corners and then not actually doing the work. Either way, it's a matter of having or adopting a growth mindset, giving it a try and using that positive mindset that I've talked about in earlier chapters. You'll have more insight into your thinking patterns and drive, which will influence your current behaviour. But keep practicing and applying new approaches using the Scenario Thinking Framework™ for best outcomes. Surprise yourself.

In the next chapter, we'll be talking about four neuroscience hacks to help set yourself up for success.

7

FOUR NEUROSCIENCE HACKS TO SET YOU UP FOR SUCCESS

What is neuroscience? According to the University of Oxford behavioural neuroscience department, it is "the study of the brain mechanisms underlying behaviour, which helps to understand how the normal brain works to support cognition, emotion and sensorimotor function." Don't worry. This chapter is not academic or scientific (although I love reading about this, so maybe that's what my next book will be about). In Chapter 4, we already touched on what happens in the brain when we get into a "flow" state. But it is good to know how neuroscience fits in with new approaches because that understanding will set you up for success. "To hack" is slang or informal language for "to change something" and, in the context of this chapter, to make things work better for you.

There are many neuroscience hacks you can use to set yourself up for success. For simplicity's sake, I've chosen four, which are the ones I also use with my coachees after I have made them aware of their strengths. These help to enhance their productivity and performance and improve how they start their day.

They are called "neuroscience" hacks because what you're doing is trying to control your mind and exert more control over what you're saying to yourself. In previous chapters, I've explained what happens in your brain with the release of neurotransmitters and neurochemicals like dopamine. They all effect your brain functions. But, when we encounter change or adversity, one of the effects on your brain is "fight, flight or freeze." That instinctive response gets in the way of trying something new; it prevents you from making changes because they feel risky. Or simply it can prevent you from thinking clearly. In business, there's not much life-threatening danger around us, but there are new or challenging ideas and people that can trigger our "fight, flight or freeze" response. To set yourself up for success, you need to calm your mind to regain the overview, think on your feet and then use that calm state of mind to address the new demands on your radar.

JOIN THE EARLY MORNING ROUTINE - CLUB

It's not just the four hacks themselves that will make you more efficient. It's incorporating these four hacks into a personalised, combined routine. And yes, people, preferably an early morning routine. When you use this routine first thing in the morning it sets you up for success for the day. You can do these hacks anytime, anywhere. But in my experience, it is most beneficial when we do them in the morning.

I'm not alone in this recommendation. I learned and read about it from some of the world's best leaders, inspiring business greats like motivational guru Tony Robbins; founder at Virgin Group and business magnate, Richard Branson; and the podcaster, entrepreneur and author of several bestselling business books, Tim Ferris, a favourite of mine. They all have specific morning routines that they swear by. Tim's motto is, "when you win the morning, you win the day." He recommends in a podcast on morning routines to switch your phone to airplane mode before you go to sleep so that you don't wake up seeing all your new messages and emails. Then, make your bed before you leave, so that you already have a task accomplished at the beginning of your day. That sets you up psychologically to be more productive in your day. To me, that makes perfect sense. And it also works for me. These are examples of neuroscience hacks: you are tricking your brain and conditioning or priming yourself to be even more productive and effective throughout your day. You're setting the right tone.

By having these, and my four hacks in your toolbox, you give yourself an advantage in setting up a success routine that prepares you for whatever you need to face that day. In my experience and what I read in business journals and literature, I've found that the most successful people in business, elite athletes and high-performers all use a (morning) routine.

Calming your mind makes you more creative. For example, Caroline Brouwer, the elite athlete and offshore sailing world champion who I interviewed in Chapter 4, has a solid routine for every sailing race she does. She wakes up at the same time, does the same exercise, trains the same way, then she has breakfast. She dresses in the same set of fresh clothes so that she doesn't have to think about what to wear and then packs her bag. When she gets on the boat, she might take some quick notes. Then, it's the media interview and the goodbyes. She then takes five or 10 minutes for herself to visualise what's going to happen ideally on the day, and to manage any pressure she feels. She tells herself, "Now, it's getting serious, I need to focus and concentrate." Her nerves may interfere with her appetite, but her routine is to take two bananas with her to eat before the race starts, as that particular food works best for her. And with that routine, she's completely prepared to do the best sailing that she is trained to do.

INTRODUCING THE FOUR HACKS

I chose these four hacks because, when you combine them in a five- to 10-minute routine, they make a huge difference to your day. You effortlessly achieve your desired outcomes. Here, the evidence is in the doing. You need to experience it and then finetune and make it your own. Find out what works for you best.

In general, people shy away from introspection or self-reflection. They claim lack of time or motivation. Until adversity hits them and they are forced to reflect. But these four hacks are short and sweet to make them more appealing to try out. The first three hacks, which are the easiest to combine, are intention, gratitude, and mindfulness. Each takes only a few minutes. The fourth hack is exercise. You can choose the length of the workout to suit your lifestyle and capabilities. But a short routine contributes to its effectiveness because it encourages you to try it, and when you experience the benefits, you keep doing it. You notice that when you don't do it, you don't feel quite right. That will be your intrinsic motivation to do it the next day. Let's explore a bit more in detail.

HACK ONE: INTENTION

Setting intentions for each day means thinking of and visualising the challenges you might face in a day and how you're going to meet them in the best possible way. For example, say you know you're going to have a difficult conversation with somebody who might be defensive because they have been defensive in conversations that you've had before. Set an intention to bring empathy to the conversation, use your strengths, be patient and listen well. Decide you will try to understand rather than only to convey your message. Share your intention with the person you plan to speak with. Those are the kinds of intentions that you can set to bring about a positive outcome.

When you set a positive intention, you trick your brain into calming down. You tell your brain: "Calm down. Yes, I am going to do something new and out of my comfort zone, but I got this." Your stress levels will lower as you start to feel more confident. It works even when you get to the office and something unexpected happens. You tend to stick to, and more importantly, behave according to that intention. If you are late in a meeting and there's already a heated conversation going, your intention will help you remain calm and improvise a good response without too much stress. But if you haven't set an intention, you tend to become more reactive.

We default to negative thinking; intention setting is a way to prevent that.

Elite athletes use intention setting through visualisation. In my interview with world-class sailor, Carolijn Brouwer, she described how she visualises holding the trophy because that's what gets her through the trials and tribulations that happen during any sailing race. If you can imagine that you will achieve the goal that you are after in the end, it makes the adversity worth it.

Intention setting itself is so simple. Think about your day, and the key situations you'll be facing. Then think about achieving a positive outcome in each of those situations and consider the behaviours and strengths you can present to help reach that outcome. Make sure to articulate your intention, and say, "This is what I'm trying to make sure that I can help you with," or "I'd like to make sure I understand your point of view in our conversation." In my experience, whenever you show your genuine interest and involvement, the other person will feel more comfortable with opening up as well.

HACK TWO: GRATITUDE

Some of the coachees I work with still find the idea of practicing gratitude fluffy at the beginning, but they know that I'm not a fluffy person. I am a bit of a tomboy, and I wasn't raised with this type of language. When I first heard of it, I needed to get my head around it." Gratitude" is a neuroscience hack because you're tricking your brain, redirecting your attention into positivity by articulating something that you're grateful for. You articulate what it is you have that you are grateful for or happy with (as I adopted that in my language), or an experience that makes you grateful. We stop (for a moment) thinking about what is lacking or not going well. Gratitude releases dopamine in the brain, and that is the neurochemical associated with feeling good.

According to the Merriam-Webster dictionary, gratitude is simply the state of being grateful. That doesn't tell us much about what gratitude means within psychology and positive psychology: appreciation of what is valuable and meaningful to us. To me, gratitude is the expression of happiness that a situation is or was a certain way. It's literally saying, "I am thankful for …" or "I am grateful for…" And it can be applied to any situation.

Three weeks of gratitude training will improve personal wellbeing and overall psychological health, writes Friederike Fabritius in her book *The Leading Brain*. "An attitude of gratitude leads to an increase in energy and exercising and a boost in optimism, as well as better sleep and more time spent helping others."

Gratitude takes only a minute. It helps if you write down what you're grateful for rather than thinking about them because it cements the gratitude into your mind. It is a confidence and happiness booster. Articulate your gratitude in a bit of detail. Rather than stating that you're happy the sun is shining or that you had a good conversation with a peer or a boss today, articulate to yourself why it's meaningful to you. Is it because you were nervous about having that conversation and when you finally got the courage to have it, you were pleasantly surprised with a favourable response? That will already ignite some further thinking and inspiration. In short, it makes you feel more in control of your life—and who doesn't want that?

HACK THREE: EXERCISE

If you want mental and physical resilience, you must build exercise into your daily routine. By exercise, I don't mean exercise such as that demanded by competitive sports. I have always been engaged in sports but, probably like you, I'm not 20 anymore. And when your knees don't cooperate, you must find other ways to move and exercise and keep fit. Quick but effective exercise can come in any form, from going to the gym through to swimming, or yoga or just having a mat in your living room to do some regular push ups, sit-ups and stretches. The goal is to get your blood flowing and get more oxygen to your brain, whether you're doing it for five minutes or an hour.

WHY EXERCISE MATTERS

I am not writing a treatise about exercise, but I will briefly summarise the benefits. Exercise clears your mind and makes you more creative in problem-solving and decision making. Research tells us that exercise is one of the most effective defences against stress and depression. It improves your mood because it releases chemicals like endorphins and serotonin in your brain and stimulates the parts of the brain responsible for memory and learning, reducing your stress and improving mental health. Your cognitive test scores, long-term memory, reasoning, attention, problem solving, and improvisation will all improve, author Fabritius writes.

Exercise can reduce the risk of illnesses like heart and lung disease, high blood pressure, diabetes, obesity, cancer, dementia, Alzheimer's disease and Parkinson's disease. It can help you improve fitness and lose weight, which is good for your health overall and improve your self-esteem. Last but not least, exercise also helps improves your sleep, which is important in many different ways.

KEEP YOUR ROUTINE SIMPLE
It really doesn't need to be too complicated or time consuming, but it must be regular. A daily 20-minute walk is fabulous.

Daily
My daily 12-minute morning routine is:

- Intention setting—two minutes
- Gratitude—two minutes
- Mindfulness - two minutes
- Exercise: stretching—kettlebell swings (weights) and sit/push-ups—six minutes.

Weekly
Two to three days a week, I schedule time in the morning for:

- training at the gym, or
- for a long walk outside.

I'm human, so I don't feel like going to the gym every day. But the 10-minute morning routine is a daily commitment that makes me feel refreshed and accomplished. I also drink several glasses of water first thing in the morning, that refreshes and resets my whole system. And yes, we are a whole system, not just a body with brains. We are made up of a complex combination of inner selves, our social and professional environment, our values, and the values, culture and systems of the organisation we work in. So, make sure you are aware of and combine all those elements well, when you strive to be your most effective self.

HACK 4: MINDFULNESS

Mindfulness has its roots in Buddhist meditation. It's now widely accepted as a stress management technique because of the many positive effects that it has on both mind and body. It's a way of paying purposeful attention to the present moment by focusing on your breathing and letting your thoughts come and go while practicing being non-judgmental. Mindfulness produces a calming effect on your mind and lets you refocus. It revitalises you and allows you to see what is important.

Leaders who I work with are exposed to changing, fast-paced environments. From time to time they become overwhelmed by all the problems they need to solve. They struggle with information overload. Sometimes they just can't see where they should start addressing their problems. They struggle with time management and priorities. They get frustrated. And they say to themselves, "Oh, I wish I had more rest or time to think."

One of the quickest ways to get that space in your mind again is to practice mindfulness. Knowing when to reset yourself is only half the solution. Practising mindfulness for a few minutes in the morning, and even throughout the day, will make you more effective and doesn't cost anything. According to journalist Tom Ireland in his article in *Scientific American Magazine*, June 12th, 2014, "What does mindfulness meditation do to your brain?": "brain imaging techniques are revealing that this ancient practice can profoundly change the way different regions of the brain communicate with each other—and therefore how we think—permanently. A MRI scan shows that after an eight-week course of mindfulness practice, the amygdala, which is the brain's fight-or-flight response centre, appears to shrink. The connection between the amygdala and the rest of the brain gets weaker, while the connection between areas associated with attention and concentration gets stronger." How fascinating, right? Scientists now call this capability neuroplasticity: the amazing capacity to change and reorganise synaptic connections, often in response to learning or following injury.

When you practise mindfulness, you start to recognise when to step back from a stressful situation better. You will increase your ability to imagine new ways to combine your strengths and achieve a new solution. You also start to make connections between situations you might not have thought connected previously—to think outside the box. Or, as journalist Tom Ireland further states, "In other words, our more primal responses to stress seem to be superseded by more thoughtful ones."

Mindful between meetings

When I discuss the benefits of mindfulness with my coachees, they tell me they walk from one meeting to the next, almost running to get there on time. How can they be mindful? Here is a mindfulness trick: look up, instead of ahead. If you look ahead, you'll see other people (also running to their next meeting, which can add to the stress). If you look up a little bit, there's a sense of calm. All you see is blank walls or the ceiling, or the blue sky. (I know what I would prefer.) Use your peripheral vision to not let all those details over-stimulate your brain. Focus on your breath as you walk. Take a deep breath in, and a long breath out. It's also a good tool for anger management, or when you're in a work situation where you're upset or nervous. You will be astonished at how this little mindfulness exercise calms the mind so you can handle situations better.

Mini-meditation moments

Some people might say, "I'm not a morning person," "I don't have time" or "I have kids and I need to do the school run." I say, it's just a couple of minutes. You get up at six and you argue that's early enough. But to get up at five to six isn't much of a change.

It doesn't have to be in the morning. Choose a different time or practice mindfulness throughout your day—a minute or two here and there—because there are so many moments during the day that you can find yourself in information overload.

Tami Roos, an American meditation facilitator and author based in Australia, who has a PhD from the American Institute of Holistic Theology, showed me a simple exercise at a female entrepreneurs retreat in Fiji last year. I'd like to share it with you as I use it all the time. Many of my coachees have adopted it in their routine, too.

Count your breaths starting from 10 and working back to zero. Count three times 10 on the inhale and three times 10 on the exhale, then three times nine on the inhale and three times nine on the exhale. By the time you reach zero, you're quite relaxed. Sometimes, I don't even get as far as five before I am relaxed. Because I have been concentrating on breathing and counting at the same time, it has already taken my mind off my stresses. It only takes you a minute to do that exercise. There are many more simple mindfulness techniques out there. It doesn't have to be complicated.

Another interesting assessment tool I can mention here, is the Global Leadership and Wellbeing Survey (GLWS), which is a self-assessment that focuses on how well you balance your energy towards your life and your work. This tool helps to gain greater insights into what's driving leaders' performance and wellbeing. The result of the assessments helps to redirect the focus to the work or life situation that needs the attention, that will balance work-life better and channel your energy and effort on the right focus areas. It's helpful to clear your mind and practice mindfulness around these situations.

Keep it up

Discipline is an important part of mindfulness. In my experience, coachees who try it out notice a change. When they stop doing it for whatever reason, they notice the difference and get back into it. Once you've experienced the upside, it's easier to remind yourself and keep up the discipline to practice regularly. You don't have to do it every day—it's particularly useful for those days when you feel a bit restless or anxious. Routine is good and gives a sense of direction, but sometimes we can't stick to it, or we forget to do it or we're resistant to doing it. Pick it up again the next day. For a small investment of time, you will be much more productive—a big return on investment

CHAPTER CONCLUSION

Take a small investment of time and put these four hacks together into a routine that works for you. They are intention, gratitude, exercise and mindfulness. Get into the habit of doing that routine because it really makes a difference to your day and sets you up for success. It's quite contagious. My coachees have already passed it on to their loved ones, kids and colleagues. One coachee even takes it a step further and does mindfulness exercises with their team at the start of their working day.

When you read through the four hacks you might think, "is that all?" and "how will these small, subtle changes make a difference?" Make no mistake, all four hacks and the tools in this book, combined, will make a massive different. See for yourself.

I hope that after reading this chapter, you're curious to try it out. Mix it up and find out what works for you. This is not a set routine that you have to do. You can change the sequence and do more or less of something. Just see what makes it worthwhile for you. Notice what happens at the end of the day, how you feel, what you achieved, and then tailor your own routine to suit your ideal outcomes.

FINAL NOTE FROM THE AUTHOR

When was the last time you encountered adversity? I bet you the timing couldn't have been worse, and you soon realised you couldn't ignore it. You had to deal with it, sooner rather than later, if only to keep your sanity. I truly hope my book will help you next time, in navigating through the adversity and turning it into an advantage.

"Only accept the status quo that's right for you."

You have more choice and control in dealing with adversity than you might think at first. I hope I have encouraged you to start using the Scenario Thinking Framework™ whenever you can imagine that your status quo can be so much better. Enjoy anticipating, preparing and actioning your next steps for outcomes that work best for you, and the time and energy saved. The goal of this book is to help you minimise your efforts, and maximise your peak performance, and that of your team, whilst having fun and fulfilment.

"If you keep doing the same thing, you keep getting the same outcomes."

You will be going out of your comfort zone at first, but I really hope you will try out new approaches, and surprise yourself by what you are capable of. In working with my coachees I have seen leaders become unstuck where they were stuck in their procrastination. Where they assumed they couldn't get buy-in for their project, they got it. Where they lacked self-belief that they could position themselves for their next level role or even turn around a seemingly difficult conversation to a positive one, they were successful in achieving those outcomes. The secret of their success? They increased their awareness, had a growth mindset and were willing to give the Scenario Thinking Framework™ a go.

Like the shampoo commercial says: "You're worth it." Allow yourself time to keep having the overview and reflect and reset regularly. It all starts with having the bigger picture. When adversity hits you and you find yourself acting again like a true high achiever, just pushing through, remember what you can do to shift back to high performance mode. Remind yourself of your strengths and values when you use the Scenario Thinking Framework™, and use them more, or less, whichever is required. Give yourself some slack and come out stronger.

Mastering the Scenario Thinking Framework™ is a work in progress, especially as we're continuously evolving whilst anticipating and creating the next steps of being our best selves. I'm keen to hear how you are setting yourself up for success and which morning routine you have come up with, to fly through your day and any adversity that might come your way. It's only work, not real life or death issues, so make sure to trick your brain out of freezing, and deal with adversity head on.

Now, don't laugh but, the irony is that adversity hit me again just before finalising this book: in the last weeks of working on this book, I was very much in flow, feeling the right amount of deadline pressure, whilst also having a great week of coaching conversations with my coachees, and about to enjoy a long weekend away in Queensland, when concussion number four happened. Nothing serious, but the timing is absolutely hilarious, yet very unwanted as you can imagine.

Now I need to role model my brave face again and practise what I preach. I'm turning it into an advantage. And hey, if I can do it, you can do it.

I'm keen to hear from you and what your journey and examples are with adversity. Wishing you good luck and feel free to follow me on LinkedIn or my website for more stories and new-found wisdom about managing and maximising your peak performance through adversity.

For more information, feel free to reach out via:
www.lantoscoaching.com
https://www.linkedin.com/in/claudia-lantos/

ABOUT THE AUTHOR

No-one likes adversity and Claudia Lantos is no exception. But while the bad times are never embraced at first, adversity has enabled Claudia to reinvent herself several times to her advantage. Over a period of around 10 years, adversity struck Claudia in the form of five car accidents—of one which took her about nine months to recover from—and three concussions from sailing accidents while building her coaching business in The Netherlands and later in Australia. Claudia has turned these hard knocks into brilliant insights for her clients and an advantageous mindset for herself. This book sums up her learnings to give anyone who wants to turn adversity to their advantage new approaches, to tackle anything that is thrown at them and come out stronger.

Combining her psychological and coaching training with her corporate executive search and legal background, Claudia has built excellent insight into corporate dynamics, leadership development and behavioural issues, servicing a wide range of organisations. In the last 25 years, Claudia prides herself in having worked with executive leaders and continued to consult them, through the bigger part of their careers.

As a former national-level sports enthusiast at karate and offshore sailing, and accredited in organisational coaching, she is specialised in executive coaching for high performers in leadership roles, focused on a strengths-based, behavioural change and growth mindset approach, using the adult learning principles of positive psychology.

Claudia started her career as a Lawyer in Labour Law and IP in The Netherlands, Europe in 1993, and she has been a member of country management teams based in Amsterdam and Singapore for a UK-listed professional services group, setting up new business service offerings and building and managing small teams. She successfully led her own executive coaching and executive search business in the Netherlands for eight years, before settling down in Bondi Beach, Australia in 2012.

LIST OF RESOURCES

CHAPTER 1

1. *The Cambridge Dictionary*: Definition of noun adversity: "Adversity is a difficult or unlucky situation or event."

2. Tony Robbins, *Awaken the Giant Within*, Pocket Books 2001. "How we deal with adversity in challenges will shape our lives more than almost anything else."

3. The Round Britain and Ireland Race: Comparable to Royal Ocean Racing Club annual offshore sailing race held in spring. The race I participated in was organised by Challenge Business, an company started by Sir Chay Blyth in 1989, known for their Global Challenge race around the world with a fleet of 72ft one design steel yachts, crewed by ordinary people, no elite sailors, and was unique as it took the west about route around Britain and Ireland against prevailing winds and currents.

4. Rafael Nadal: Spanish professional tennis player, ranked world No. 2 in men's single tennis by the Association of Tennis Professionals (ATP).

5. Robert Downey Jr. American actor and singer known from *Iron Man*, *Avengers and Sherlock Holmes*.

6. Keanu Reeves: Canadian Actor, director, producer and musician, known for his movies *John Wick*, *Point Break* and *The Matrix*.

7. Steve Jobs : Chairman, CEO and co-founder of Apple during 1997 till 2011.

8. Arianna Huffington: American Greek syndicated columnist and business women: founder of The Huffington Post, founder and CEO of Thrive Global and author of 15 books.

9. Oprah Winfrey: American media executive, actress talk show host, television producer and philanthropist, best known for her talk show *The Oprah Winfrey Show* during 1986 to 2011.

10. VUCA stands for: Volatile, Uncertain, Complex and Ambiguity—used in business publications.

11. The SCARF model of behaviour: first published by David Rock in 2008, article in cleverism.com in 2016

12. Brene Brown: American research professor in The Graduate College of Social Work at the University of Houston: "You can choose courage or you can choose comfort, but you can't have both."

13. J.K Rowling: British novelist, philanthropist, film producer, television producer and screenwriter, best known for the Harry Potter novels and series, as mentioned in Jeff Haden's article on Inc. about female founders.

14. Charles Darwin: English naturalist, geologist and biologist, best known for his contributions to the science of evolution: "It's not the strongest of species that survive nor the most intelligent, but the ones most responsive to change."

15. Carol Dweck: professor of Psychology at Stanford University, known for her work on the mindset psychological trait: "Fixed vs Growth mindset."

16. Kaizen theory: Kaizen is the Japanese word for "improvement." Kaizen is an approach to create continuous improvement, based on the idea that small, ongoing positive changes can reap major improvements.

17. Tony Robbins: Goalcast video from 22 February 2018 posted on Facebook

18. Marshall Goldsmith: *What Got You Here, Won't Get You There* book on leadership, published by Hyperion in 2007

19. Victor Frankl: bestselling book: *Man's Search for Meaning*, first published in 1959, under a different title. *Life is Never Made Unbearable by Circumstances, but Only by Lack of Meaning and Purpose.*

20. Leah Weiss, PhD, MSW: author, teacher researcher and meditation expert at Stanford University specialising in the application of mindfulness quoted Victor Frankl's work during TEDxTraverseCity Talk.

21. Desmond Tutu: South African cleric and theologian known for his work as an anti-apartheid and human rights activist.

22. Ruth Bader Ginsburg: Associate Justice of the Supreme Court of the United States and activist for equality of rights for women

23. Beyoncé: American singer songwriter, actress, record producer and dancer, who rose to fame in the late 1990's as lead singer for the R&B girl group Destiny's Child.

24. Amy Wrzesniewski: Yale School of Management researcher, on purpose.

CHAPTER 2

1. "The strategic planning" method: used by some organisations to make flexible, long-term plans, is in large part an adaption and generalisation of a classic method used by military intelligence.

2. "Design thinking": is more relevant to the innovation of new products or sources, and refers to cognitive, strategic, and principle processes by which design concepts are developed by designers or design teams.

3. Steven Kotler: New York Times-bestselling author book *The Rise of Superman*, published by Quercus in 2015.

4. Mark Setton, D.Phil., co-founder and CEO of Pursuit of Happiness and Paul Desan, MD, Ph.D., co-founder of Pursuit of Happiness and the Director of the Psychiatric Consultation Service for Yale New Haven Hospital, on Positive psychology: a scientific study of human flourishing and an applied approach to optimal functioning.

5. Abraham Maslow psychologist in the 1950's, originally coined the term "Positive Psychology." He used the term somewhat loosely to call for a more balanced view of human nature, that is, to draw attention to human potentialities as well as psychological afflictions.

6. Martin Seligman: American psychologist, educator and author of self-help books. He popularised Positive Psychology in 2002 through his influential work *Authentic Happiness*, defining it as the study of positive emotions and the "strengths that enable individuals and communities to thrive." Positive Psychology is largely focused on the study of positive emotions and "signature strengths."

CHAPTER 3

1. Elon Musk: CEO of Tesla who was reportedly, when he is stressed, sleeping on his factory floor as he thinks he doesn't have time to go home, shower and recharge. The point he made in the CBS interview with Gayle King.

2. Joseph M Juran: Management Consultant who suggested The Pareto Principle: also known as the 80/20 rule, the law of the vital few or the principle of factor sparsity, and named it after Italian economist Vilfredo Pareto. For more information, read the article "The 80/20 Rule And How It Can Change Your Life" by Kevin Kruse: https://www.forbes.com/sites/kevinkruse/2016/03/07/80-20-rule/#23a9bfae3814

3. Dr. Maxwell Maltz: American, international bestselling author of classic "Psycho-Cybernetics," a self-help book from 1960, that has inspired and enhanced the lives of more than 30 million readers

4. Tony Robbins: (From *Unlimited Power*, self-help book published by Fawcett Columbine in 1987) describes Maltz' book in a great way, using my favourite metaphor sailing: https://www.dymocks.com.au/book/psycho-cybernetics-and-updated-and-expanded-by-maxwell-maltz-9780399176135

CHAPTER 4

1. Carolijn Brouwer: Volvo Ocean Race veteran and Rolex World Sailor of the Year 2018, who features in my interview with her in chapter 4.

2. Jamie Wheal: co-founder and Executive Director of the Flow Genome Project, expert on Peak Performance and leadership, specialises in the neuroscience and application of Flow states. He explains Flow brilliantly in a YouTube video published on Dec 26, 2013 which is called: "Hacking the GENOME of Flow: Jamie Wheal at TEDxVeniceBeach."

3. Jamie Wheal: also mentions the phrase "Transient Hypofrontality" If you like to see Jamie's YouTube video, and I can highly recommend it, this is the link: https://www.youtube.com/watch?v=WqAtG77JjdM

4. Steven Kotler: co-founder and Director of Research for the Flow Genome Project, describes flow in his New York Times bestselling book *The Rise of Superman*. This becomes even more apparent in his video "Maximum performance with the Flow Cycle youtube video: https://youtu.be/v9DJqcTsHNY

5. Friederike Fabritius, MS: German author and leading expert in the field of Neuroleadership and Hans W. Hagemann, PHD, German author and Managing Partner and co-founder of the global management consultancy Munich Leadership Group (MLG): *The Leading Brain, neuroscience hacks to work smarter, better, happier*, published by Penguin/Random House 2017, describe in their book that "without fun, Peak Performance is practically impossible." They mention "DNA of Peak Performance: Dopamine, Noradrenaline and Acetylcholine."

6. Jamie Wheal: whom I introduced earlier as a Peak Performance expert, states that there are four states in which you tend to go in and out of: Struggle, Release, Flow and Recovery state.

7. Dr Tasha Eurich: organisational psychologist, researcher and NY Times bestselling author, states in her article on HBR.org, "What Self Awareness Really is (and How to Cultivate it)" published on January 04, 2018, she quotes research that suggests that "when we see ourselves clearly, we are more confident and more creative. We make sounder decisions, build stronger relationships, and communicate more effectively. We're less likely to lie, cheat, and steal. We are better workers who get more promotions. And we're more effective leaders with more satisfied employees and more profitable companies."

8. Chris Smith: Founder and CEO of Athlete Network gave an interview to the American magazine Entrepreneur in 2015, https://www.entrepreneur.com/article/244920 , where he talked about the five things athletes apply well, that can teach entrepreneurs about overcoming adversity. It's called "5 Things About Overcoming Adversity That Athletes Can Teach Entrepreneurs."

9. Carolijn Brouwer: Dutch elite Sailor, 2018 Rolex World Sailor of the Year, Twice ISAF (International Sailing Federation) World Sailor of the Year Award Winner Volvo Ocean Race, four times World Champion, Sports Women of the Year 2018 WISP (World of Women in Sports, for elite athletes) three times Olympic Games, three times Volvo Ocean Race, Winner of the 2017-2018 Volvo Ocean Race with Dongfeng Race Team, as the first women to win the race, and Helmsman for the Wild Oats X or Ocean Respect Sailing, an all-female team in The Sydney-Hobart Race of 2018, finishing 2nd on handicap and 6th on line honours, all whilst spreading the message of sustainability and care for our oceans.

10. Thomas Edison: American inventor in fields like electric power generation, mass communication and sound recording - and business man, who has been described as America's greatest inventor, quotes "Many of life's failures are people who did not realise how close they were to success when they gave up."

11. Warren Buffett: CEO at Berkshire Hathaway, American business magnate, investor, speaker and philanthropist and one of the world's wealthiest men, with a net worth of 85 billion USD at 88 years, quoted "It takes 20 years to build a reputation and five minutes to ruin it. If you think about that, you'll do things differently."

12. Cynthia Measom: a Texas-based writer and editor specialised in personal finance and business wrote the article: "How to Make Proactive Decisions." https://smallbusiness.chron.com/make-proactive-decisions-49754.html , she said: "If you are active rather than passive in the workplace or if you take the initiative to prepare for events rather than react to them, you are likely a proactive decision-maker."

CHAPTER 5

1. Shawn Anchor, American author and speaker known for his advocacy of positive psychology and Michelle Gielan, American researcher and bestselling author, researcher and speaker for the Institute of Applied Positive Research, published their article in HBR on June 24, 2016, "Resilience is about how you recharge and not how you endure," in which they describe that there is a direct scientific correlation between lack of recovery and increased incidence of health and safety problems.

2. Arianna Huffington: American Greek author, describes in her book *The Sleep Revolution* that sacrificing sleep for the sake of productivity actually leads to 11 days lost productivity per year per worker, or about $2,280.

3. Jim Loehr and Tony Schwartz: The New York Times bestselling authors, have contributed to this topic in this book's Chapter 5, in their book *The power of full engagement: Managing energy, not time, is the key to high performance and personal renewal* by stating that "if you spend too much time in the performance zone, you need more time in the recovery zone, otherwise you risk burnout."

4. Tony Robbins: Article and story on his website www.tonyrobbins.com: "Say goodbye to stress: How to recognise burnout symptoms before it's too late."

5. Simon Sinek: well-known author, thought leader and speaker always states: "Start with why."

6. *Psychology Today*: magazine published every two months in the United States since 1967, published this article from 6 April 2011: "Under Pressure: your brain on conflict" on how cortisol, that is released in our brain when under stress, affects our memories.

7. Friederike Fabritius, MS and Hans M. Hagemann, PHD: German authors of *The Leading Brain*.

8. Dr. David Rock: Director of the NeuroLeadership Institute, created and developed The SCARF model—in 2008—which uses neuroscience to effectively lead and work with others.

9. Marie Kondo: Japanese organising consultant and author on her KonMari method, with a series of shows on Netflix in 2019 has written books like, *The Life-Changing Magic of Tidying Up* in 2011, which has been published in more than 30 countries and *Spark Joy*.

10. Diane Kucala: American author, founder and Chief Leadership Officer of Blueprint Leadership describes in her Huffington Post article https://www.huffingtonpost.com/great-work-cultures/leading-by-example-a-guid_b_7270048.html, "Leading by Example: A Guide to Self-Management" published on 05/12/2015 07:06 pm ET and Updated Dec 06, 2017, in which she describes self-management as "an individual demonstrating self-control and an ability to manage time, priorities and decision-making capacity, creating a more effective leadership style."

CHAPTER 6

1. Dennis Saleebey, Charles Rapp & Anne Weick: the team that used a strengths-based approach in social work, formally developed from the University of Kansas. In 1997, Charles Rapp wrote *The Strengths Model*, which focused on "amplifying the well part of the patient." The popularity of his approach spread quickly and in 1999, Dr. Martin Seligman, the president of the American Psychological Association at the time, made an observation that fuelled strength-based practice.

2. Marcus Buckingham and Donald Clifton: introduced the strengths perspective to the business world in 1995. American, educational Psychology Professor Donald Clifton and founder of Selection Research Incorporated (SRI) helping organisations with employee selection, recruited Marcus Buckingham. After SRI acquired The Gallup Organisation in 1988, Clifton became Chairman and Gallup expanded beyond public opinion polls. It became known for management consulting business, consulting companies on ways to improve their businesses by homing in on their employees' strengths. In 1999 Clifton created the online assessment tool Clifton StrengthsFinder (now known as CliftonStrengths) that focuses on 34 themes that make up the user's personality.

3. Ekaterina Walter: American author of the Wall street Journal bestseller *Think like Zuck* (2013) and coauthor of *The Power of Visual Storytelling* (2015) and Forbes contributor describes the notion of strength-based leadership and therefore strength-based coaching is outlined by her in an article in Forbes in 2013, https://www.forbes.com/sites/ekaterinawalter/2013/08/27/four-essentials-of-strength-based-leadership/#4d8377d464c9, titled "Four Essentials of Strength-Based Leadership."

4. The Leadership Circle: Professional Training and Coaching Company, created and developed The Leadership Circle Profile LCP, see website www.leadershipcircle.com.

CHAPTER 7

1. University of Oxford explains behavioural neuroscience as: "the study of the brain mechanisms underlying behaviour, which helps to understand how the normal brain works to support cognition, emotion and sensorimotor function." https://www.psych.ox.ac.uk/research/behavioural-cognitive-neuroscience.

2. Inspiring business greats like Tony Robbins, Richard Branson, and also the podcaster, entrepreneur and author of several bestselling business books, Tim Ferris, well known for his books *The Four-Hour Work Week*, *Tools for Titans* and *Tribe of Mentors*.

3. Merriam-Webster dictionary: gratitude is simply the state of being grateful. And that doesn't tell us much about what gratitude means within psychology and positive psychology, but it is more or less appreciation of what is valuable and meaningful to one. And it represents a general state of thankfulness.

4. Friederieke Fabritius: author of earlier mentioned book *The Leading Brain*, states that the benefits "of just three weeks of gratitude training has been shown to improve personal wellbeing and overall psychological health. It leads to an increase in energy and exercising and a host in optimism, as well as better sleep and more time spent helping others."

5. *The Scientific American Magazine*: describes in an article on June 12th, 2014, Neuroscientific insights, "brain imaging techniques are revealing that this ancient practice can profoundly change the way different regions of the brain communicate with each other—and therefore how we think—permanently. The article is called "What does mindfulness meditation do to your brain?" https://blogs.scientificamerican.com/guest-blog/what-does-mindfulness-meditation-do-to-your-brain/

6. Tami Roos: American meditation facilitator and author, based in Australia, who has a PhD from the American Institute of Holistic Theology,

7. Audrey McGibbon and Karen Gillespie: Psychologists and authors of the Global Leadership and Wellbeing Survey (GLWS) and founders of EEK & Sense, describe the assessment tool GLWS as a "uniquely holistic, evidence-based tool that delivers deep insights into what shapes and sustains a leader's success, at work and at home."

NOTES